CANA REVISITED

By the same author:

To Be a Christian (The Canterbury Press Norwich, 1994)
Sharing the Faith (CLA, 1988)

CANA REVISITED

– a personal pilgrimage

JOHN BARNES

The Canterbury Press
Norwich

FOR

MY FORMER PARISHIONERS

AND OTHER FRIENDS

CONTENTS

INTRODUCTION

LAST SUNDAY I left my parish. Not to move to another one, and not because I had reached retiring age (I'm forty-nine), but because, somewhat to my surprise, I had resigned the living over a matter of conviction. I had been the Anglican parish priest at Wymondham, an old market town in Norfolk for over five years, and I had expected to remain there for considerably longer. It is a parish which has enjoyed long incumbencies this century – no less than three of them lasting over twenty years – and when the bishop had first asked me to go there he had said explicitly that he wanted me to stay there for some time. But after Evensong last Sunday, July 31st, a 'farewell' Evensong, followed by speeches and a presentation made in a swelteringly hot church hall, I drove away from the parish for the last time.

It's easy to say simply that I had left my parish behind me. But saying that is only to use a kind of shorthand for something quite complex and so far as I am concerned fairly fundamental to my way of living and indeed thinking. What precisely was I driving away from last Sunday evening? On the most basic and materialistic level – and most of us are more the animal than the angel – I was leaving my home. A home to which I'd maybe become excessively attached, but to those who know it, understandably so. It has been the Vicarage since the sixteenth-century and having been partially destroyed by fire and rebuilt in the early seventeenth-century, remodelled in the late eighteenth-century, and extended at the beginning of this century, it is full of character. The rooms are light and spacious, the curved staircase is very elegant, and the white-painted panelling in the drawing room gives the room a wonderfully comfortable and established feeling. The house, despite being almost in

the centre of an old market town, is surrounded by a
large walled garden, the walls covered with rambling
roses. A lavender hedge divides the croquet lawn from
the kitchen garden, and at the centre of the garden is an
old mulberry tree, dating maybe from soon after the
house was first built, and despite being only a part of its
former size, still yielding a fine crop of mulberries each
year to be used for summer puddings and the making of
mulberry gin!

I was also, I realised, leaving a no less delectable
church. Wymondham Abbey, consisting of the nave,
aisles and towers of a former Benedictine abbey church,
is remarkable. Outside, it is immensely impressive even
if decidedly odd. The fact that the monastic choir was
demolished at the time of the dissolution means that the
former central tower, now roofless, is at one end of the
present building, whilst the huge west tower, which was
never finished, stands at the other. The whole presents
a standing 'U' shape. Perhaps the word beautiful cannot
be used for the outside, but it certainly must be used for
the interior. I remember how as a boy I used to look
through a book of my father's called *English Cathedrals
and Abbeys*, and how I always turned to the full-page
photograph of the Nave at Wymondham, thinking that
this, of all the other abbeys and cathedrals, was the one
that I liked most. At that time I had no idea even of
where Wymondham Abbey was, let alone that I would
ever be responsible for its care. But now having lived
and worked there I can appreciate why it is that the
nave is so unusual and so attractive: it is the unlikely
combination of the twelfth-century arcades, the great
fifteenth-century 'angel' roof, and the wonderfully delicate Altar Screen, a masterpiece of Sir Ninian Comper
which glitters with burnished gold and dates from our
own century – it is the combination of these three very
different elements which makes the nave at Wymondham
so striking and so memorable.

A few weeks ago the bishop of Norwich came to the
Abbey to conduct a Confirmation. After the Service, as
he and I prepared to follow the people across to the hall

for refreshments, he looked back down the nave and asked 'John, what will you miss most about Wymond-ham?' Knowing my passion for historic buildings, and my involvement with them as, until recently, Chairman of the Diocesan Advisory Committee for the Care of Churches, I think he expected me to say 'the Abbey'. But happily I was able to reply, with complete honesty and sincerity, that what I would miss most would be the people – my parishioners. For always to the priest the people in his spiritual care are, and must be, more sig-nificant than a comfortable home to live in, and more important than a fine and historic church building to worship in. They are certainly his responsibility in spiritual terms. But more than that they are, in a sense, his family, and this most particularly if he is a celibate priest, as I am. The hope of a priest is that he will love his people, and not just those who are friendly and con-vivial but rather every member of the family which is the local church. He prays for grace to do this. And in return he receives – however undeserved – the love of his parishioners. Last Sunday, as I left my parish, I was deeply aware of how much love and understanding I had received recently. It was just over a month ago that I announced my resignation, making public the fact that I was leaving not only my parish but the Church of England in order to become a Roman Catholic. During that month no one had 'laid into me' as I had expected. I knew that many parishioners were puzzled by what I was doing, but no one expressed any kind of resentment or censure. Only sympathy and support. And now, on this last Sunday, kind things had been said, cards and presents had been handed to me, and the parish had presented me with an extraordinarily generous cheque. Here were very tangible proofs of the affection of the parishioners for their parish priest. It was these kind, generous-hearted people, friends and fellow-members of the Christian community in which I had worshipped and ministered for five years, that it was most difficult to leave behind last Sunday. And compared with them, the house, church building, and the regular pay-cheque from which I was parting seemed almost irrelevant. My sadness in leaving was very definitely centred upon the people I was saying goodbye to.

And then of course I was leaving the Church of England behind, the irritating, lovable, infuriating and, as I have come to feel, the ultimately unsatisfactory Church of England. I suppose it is very difficult for me to realise just what a formative and indeed dominant part the Church of England has played in my life up to now. It has moulded as well as supported me, and I am anxious not to leave it with any hard or ungrateful feelings. My parents had been brought up as practising Anglicans, byt well before the time of their marriage they had lapsed from active church membership, so that my first experience of Christian worship, at about the age of five or six, was when my uncle and aunt used to collect me each Sunday to take me to the Anglican parish church which they attended. All that I can now remember of it are the boiled sweets I was given to eat during the sermon, and being fascinated by the gold stars painted on the blue chancel ceiling. Since, as, I realised later, the tradition of that particular church was extreme evangelical, these two things were probably the only ones likely to appeal to the senses. Later, my parents thought that I ought to attend Sunday School, as they had done when children, and soon after it was decided that I should also join the church choir, again, as my father had done when he was a boy. Thereafter my parents became involved in church life, my father eventually becoming a Churchwarden, and my mother a highly successful (if somewhat unconventional) leader of a large infants' Sunday School. Our family life – I have no brothers or sisters – became very much church-orientated, based upon a local parish church with an old-fashioned 'middle of the road' tradition. I suppose it was when I was about twelve that I felt I would like to be a priest. As always in my life, I drifted towards this, led I hope by the Holy Spirit, who seems to work as often by nudging and easing as by catapulting. My original motives for seeking ordination were, I now realise, dubious. The clerical life seemed secure, stable, and able to provide one relatively easily with an assured place in society, a pleasant home, adequate income, plus congenial and not over-demanding work. In self-defence, I believe that I had these dubious motives simply because I didn't then know enough about God, the Faith, and the Church to be able to embrace any higher ones. Often, I think, God takes what is unworthy and in the course of time purifies and enhances it. He deals with us in somewhat unlikely ways, but always with a sureness, and lightness, of touch.

From these beginnings in the Church of England I went in time to university, choosing what was still at that time the intensely Anglican milieu of St David's College, Lampeter, and going from there to read for a second degree at St Chad's College, Durham, then still a bastion of the Anglo-Catholicism which I had first encountered at Lampeter, and which had made religion seem for the first time something vital, exciting and, ultimately, real. My chosen subject for post-graduate work was seventeenth-century Anglican thought, and I have always felt that it was from this source, from the writings of Hooker, Andrewes, Taylor, and above all Thorndike, that I learnt Catholic doctrine as opposed to Catholic practice and devotion. Theological College followed (St Stephen's House, Oxford), leading on to curacies in the Newcastle and St Asaph dioceses. And then, before my five-year incumbency at Wymondham, a twelve-year incumbency at Walsingham in North Norfolk. For virtually all my life, therefore, I have been firmly ensconced in the bosom of the Church of England, and furthermore in very good and pleasant places, taught, guided, supported, nurtured by devout and kind people. After God and my parents I owe everything, I suppose, to the Church of England. It has given me the Christian Faith, work to do within the Kingdom of God, and in material terms, a livelihood. Within it too I have found friendship, kindness, generosity and love, and I have encountered and been inspired by men and women of true holiness. Now I have left this church to which I owe so many things. It too was part of what I was leaving behind as I drove away from Wymondham last Sunday evening.

* * *

For several years now St John's account of Our Lord's first miracle, the changing of water into wine at Cana in Galilee, has held a special place in my imagination and indeed in my whole understanding of the Christian revelation. I've found this incident, with those details of it which St John chooses to record, seems to provide a key to much that is vital and I believe that St John's particular placing of it suggests that he too considered it to be of crucial importance. I think that the incident gives us the same kind of profound insight into the love of the divine Son which the Parable of the Prodigal Son gives into the love of the Father, and I believe that the incident teaches us much about the salvific process of redemption and sanctification, about the Church and about Christian discipleship. I feel that this passage from the fourth gospel speaks to me more clearly and more insistently than perhaps any other in Holy Scripture, and I feel that I have been immeasurably enriched by meditating upon it. I think it has been formative in my own spirituality, and I have wanted to have an opportunity to try and share its meaning, significance, indeed its potency, with other people.

Just such an opportunity seemed to be presenting itself when, in the weeks preceding last Sunday, I prepared to leave my parish and began to wonder how I would fill in my time during the next few months. One thing I could do, I thought, would be to try and write a little book of meditations on the Marriage at Cana. Perhaps it would never see the light of day, and that for the good reason that what I might write would not be considered worthy of publication. But perhaps I should attempt something. And then last Sunday it seemed that a spanner was being thrown into these particular works. One of our Churchwardens, who has an interest in publishing, had kindly invited me to lunch with his family on that my last day at Wymondham, and in the course of the meal he suggested that I should use the time I was now going to have available to write something about how my mind had been working during the past few months, as I had journeyed towards the decision to leave the Church of England and seek admission both to the Roman Catholic Church and, if possible, to its priesthood. I was somewhat taken aback by his suggestion; I had not entertained any thought of such a piece of writing and, as I said, I doubted whether I had anything to say which would be of any interest or value. He replied that he had been impressed by my attitude and by the way in which I had dealt with this particular crisis in my own life and in the life of the parish, and that he considered that I might well have something to say which would be useful to others in a similar situation. I felt bound to take this suggestion seriously, but I felt – with some regret – that if it seemed right to act upon it, then the idea of writing about the Marriage at Cana would have to be abandoned.

Then a day or two ago I was suddenly struck by the thought that maybe the two projects were not simply alternatives, and that it was not necessarily a case of attempting either one or the other. It occurred to me that my thinking about the difficulties which had arisen for me as regards continuing as a member of the Church of England had, to some extent, been informed at least indirectly by my understanding of that – for me – so significant passage in the fourth gospel. And certainly that the incident at Cana spoke to me insistently at this particular moment in my life, as I say goodbye to the Church in which I have ministered as a priest for nearly twenty-five years, and prepare for reception into the Roman Catholic Church. And so the idea of this book began to emerge: a book in which I do indeed meditate upon the Marriage at Cana, as I had hoped to do, but in which I also share with whoever might be interested the opinions which I have come to hold and the thoughts and feelings which I find I have at what would be, for anyone, a spiritual and vocational crossroads in their life. In many ways I hate the idea of attempting to write what must of necessity be a very personal book. I do so simply in the hope that it might help others who are perplexed by the present religious scene, and in the knowledge that the Christ who is our model and exemplar was himself ready to reveal his feelings and nature – never more so than when he turned water into wine at Cana in Galilee.

1. *On the Third Day*

I SEEM to remember reading that scholars are puzzled by the words with which St John opens his account of the Marriage at Cana. St John fails to tell us what 'the third day' relates to: what was it the third day of, or the third day after? What I think we can be sure of is that the phrase has significance; it is not a mere slip of the pen, a piece of careless writing. St John was not that kind of writer.

Perhaps the fact that a particular day is indicated serves to point us to the fact that God does not act in a random way as regards times, as if the when of a particular event is ultimately irrelevant. The writer of the Old Testament book Ecclesiastes asserts that there is a correct time for everything, and so it would seem to be with every part of the working of God. The Christian believes that the incarnation of Our Lord Jesus Christ took place in exact accordance with the divine plan, 'in the fullness of time', and that the moment when Jesus began his public ministry was not chosen in any completely arbitrary way. Similarly in this account of the Marriage at Cana, Jesus initially says to his Mother 'My hour has not yet come'. And again in his passion narrative, St John records Jesus as speaking of the hour having now come. We are given a picture of things happening according to God's foreordained plan – the plan originating in the divine wisdom – and not in some disordered, unplanned, and unforeseen way. And if God is revealed in Holy Scripture as working in this way, then we can infer that he works in just this way with us as individuals. That he knows precisely what he is doing with us and where he is leading us. That he will give us guidance and enlightenment (though never in such a way as to deprive us of his precious gift to us of freedom of will) at just the right moment, 'in the fullness of time'. The

9

Holy Spirit, Jesus promised, will lead us into truth. But we believe that this is but one aspect of the way in which Our Lord, through the Spirit, leads and directs us. It's sometimes said, and truthfully, that always the Holy Spirit is the true director of souls, leading us into holiness (which is wholeness) even as he leads us into truth. And all this in accordance with the preordained plan of God, and with everything happening just when the time is ripe. I think that St John's mention of an explicit time, a precise time – 'On the third day' – points us first to this aspect of the divine working.

Then to the Christian the mention of 'the third day' cannot fail to evoke thoughts of the resurrection of Jesus, which took place 'on the third day'. It seems that by using this phrase St John is directing our attention from the first of the great Signs, the turning of water into wine, through to the last and greatest of the Signs, the resurrection of Jesus. And indeed the very nature of this first miracle, quite apart from the opening phrase of St John's record of it, points us in that direction. In this first Sign, there is transformation and enrichment, just as there was transformation and enrichment in the crucified and risen body of Jesus – water into wine, a dead mortal body into a risen, transformed, glorified body. There is again a common changing of despair into joy, and one in which all can equally share. This first Sign seems to act as a pointer towards the ultimate victory of Christ, with St John's evocative phrase 'on the third day' serving to trigger-off our perception of this. Therefore what seems on the face of it to be an almost 'throw-away' phrase, 'On the third day' serves in fact to bring two great facts before our attention: the way in which God works in accordance with his divine plan, bringing things to be in the fullness of time, and second, the way in which all of his working points and leads forward to the glory of the resurrection, in which the whole people of God is destined to share.

*   *   *

I've just got back from my first Sunday Mass, not yet as a full member of the Catholic Church, since there is another fortnight before my Reception, but certainly as one who has now left the Church of England and who has committed himself to live and worship as a Roman Catholic. I didn't know quite how I would feel this morning, after worshipping as an Anglican Sunday by Sunday for more than forty years. In the event, I felt perfectly at home, with a true and unforced sense of peace and happiness. I felt, I suppose, that I was precisely where God meant me to be. And furthermore, that I was there at the time which he had chosen. Last Sunday, I presided at the Altar in Wymondham Abbey for the last time, and that too felt entirely (or almost entirely) right. I was, I think, where God wanted me to be last Sunday, and now I am where he wants me to be this Sunday. A matter of timing, of God's timing. The change coming, I believe and hope, just when he meant it to be in accordance with his wise, loving, and predetermined plan.

But whilst there is a right moment and a right place for something to happen – 'On the third day there was a wedding at Cana-in-Galilee' – this does not of course exclude a careful preparation being made by God. The moment of the Incarnation was prepared for by centuries of prophecy and by God's direction of the course of Israel's history. And likewise the moment of the first miracle of Jesus was prepared for by Mary becoming ready to say to Jesus 'They have no wine left' and to the servants 'Do whatever he tells you' – words which expressed the faith which had a vital part to play in the bringing about of the miracle. God's moment of action is prepared for by what is often a long and always a careful period of preparation, both of circumstances and of people. I feel that this has been the case in my own transition from Anglicanism to Catholicism. I remember looking into a Catholic church as an undergraduate, just over thirty years ago, and of feeling strangely attracted by it, and wondering whether this was for me. And again a year or two later I remember reading John Henry Newman's *Apologia Pro Vita Sua* with a feeling of expectation and of hope that I would maybe feel led to follow the path which he had taken. I think I wanted then to be converted, but in an unformed and immature way. Perhaps at that point it was simply a search for adventure, freedom, novelty. Or of that wish to be rather daring, unconventional, and 'naughty' which first led me as an undergraduate to dally with Anglo-Catholicism. Certainly, though, at that point in my life the time which God had chosen was still far distant; I was still far from having reached the third day of God's choosing.

Recently I've heard several friends who have likewise left the Church of England to become Roman Catholics say 'I wish I'd done it years ago'. I know just what they mean, and in some ways I'm tempted to feel like this myself. But I know this attitude is wrong, simply because it presupposes that the transition from the one communion to the other is merely a matter of one's own choice, of a decision which could have been taken at any time. I don't believe that it is like that, but that rather it is a matter of waiting until the will of God becomes clear, and until there is a strong (even if not overwhelming) feeling that the time – God's time – has come. Therefore I cannot regret my Anglican years, my years both as a layman and later as a priest, and consequently I cannot entertain any feeling of having wasted or misused what has realistically been the major portion of my active life. I believe that it was part of God's plan for me that I should be born into an Anglican family, that I should embrace Anglican teaching and spirituality, and eventually be ordained in the Anglican church; that I should, for nearly twenty-five years, preach and teach from an Anglican pulpit, offer the Eucharist at an Anglican altar, and bless and absolve God's people as an Anglican priest. None of this can I either regret, deny, or try to forget about. All of it is part of my spiritual pilgrimage, part of the way along which God in his wisdom and care has led me. Until the time came that the third day dawned, the time when it became clear that the transition must be made from Anglicanism to Catholicism, I believe that it was right that I should remain where God had placed me. And happily, clerical converts like myself are being encouraged to think in just this way by our superiors in the Catholic Church. We are told to give thanks for what has gone before rather than to attempt to disown or despise what is both part of us, and part of God's loving and redemptive purpose as worked out in us.

The miracle at Cana points us forward to the last and greatest of Jesus' Signs, his glorious resurrection from the dead, and for those of us who are leaving the Anglican Church to become Catholics there is undoubtedly a feeling of undergoing both death and resurrection. However much we accept and value and give thanks for our past in the way that I've been suggesting, there is still – inevitably – a sense in which we are dying to that past. There are, unavoidably, goodbyes to be said, there are real partings to make, and there are things and people, practices and attitudes, which in the course of this change of allegiance we must abandon. Dying is simply part of the way which we've got to embrace, and sometimes the experience of dying is inevitably going to be painful. There are some things – handsome houses, beautiful churches, stately liturgies, monthly pay-slips – which can tempt us not to let ourselves die, but to linger on in an unsatisfactory and unsatisfying half-life. But always the Christian knows that death is followed by resurrection, and this being so, that it is ultimately a positive and creative thing. We know too that whenever we seek to die with and for Christ, then the joy of coming-alive which will follow is out of all proportion to that which has been lost through that process of death which has preceded it. The miracle at Cana directs us towards the miracle of Easter, and in doing so it encourages us to seek that fullness of life which is what the risen Christ offers to those who follow him faithfully.

2. *There was a Wedding at Cana-in-Galilee*

THE FOURTH GOSPEL opens with St John's incomparable Prologue, and then after St John Baptist the forerunner has proclaimed Jesus to be 'the Lamb of God' and 'God's Chosen One', the Christ chooses his disciples. Then follows the account of the Marriage at Cana. So the incident which we are contemplating marks the first public appearance of Jesus the Teacher, the Healer, the performer of Signs. In neither the working of God nor in the writing of St John are circumstances and their recorded details random and devoid of meaning. Which means that the fact that the setting for the first appearance and first miracle of Jesus was a wedding cannot be irrelevant. This makes it right for us to ask what it is that is being said about the saving work of Jesus and indeed about his very nature, by the setting, the occasion, of this the first of the Signs.

Perhaps the first thing to be said about a marriage is that it marks a new beginning for the two people entering into this relationship, and some of the joy and excitement experienced at a wedding undoubtedly springs from this newness. Elsewhere in the Gospel Jesus, echoing the words of Genesis, states that in marriage two people leave behind father and mother, and cleaving to one another become 'one flesh'. Become, in effect, one new person, a new creation, a new being making a new start in God's world. Now the setting of a marriage for the first public manifestation of the Christ surely points us to the fact that he is supremely the new beginning – the new beginning for all mankind. In Baptism, as we read in the following chapter of St John's Gospel, the Christian is 'Born again'. The Christian is made new, he or she begins life afresh as a new creature alive with the risen and endless life of Our Lord Jesus Christ. Or, as St Paul expresses it by using a memorable image, the new-born

Christian becomes a 'limb' of Christ through baptism – as closely and intimately joined to him as an arm or a leg is part of the human body to which it belongs. At the new beginning which is Baptism we are indeed made 'One flesh' with Christ as truly and as surely as the two people entering into marriage are made 'One flesh'. An ancient image for the Church is 'The Bride of Christ'; it expresses the mystic union which exists between the Christ and the whole body of the Church which has been sacramentally incorporated into him, and is now alive with his endless life. Here indeed is the new beginning for mankind, as life in union with the risen Christ is made available to it. A new and life-giving beginning which is made possible by the saving work which Jesus had set out to accomplish, and which was both in a sense begun and symbolically described by the marriage at Cana.

A marriage is also, of course, about commitment: the two people entering into marriage make a solemn contract and commitment with and to one another, and this forms the foundation of that new beginning which they are making as husband and wife. They commit themselves to each other – in words familiar to Anglicans – 'till death us do part', agreeing to 'forsake all other' and to remain in the union into which they are entering whether it be 'for better or for worse, for richer or for poorer'. It is a commitment made in love, and it has something of that reckless and truly wholehearted quality with which love characteristically acts. I believe that this essential element in marriage, commitment, likewise speaks of the ministry and nature of the incarnate Word. For what is the Incarnation of Our Lord if it is not an action – indeed the supreme action – of loving commitment? In the incarnation we see the divine Word, the second person of the Holy Trinity, taking our flesh, our common humanity. We see him sharing in our very nature in order that he might redeem it. Christ the Bridegroom is made 'One flesh' with us in order that he might be the liberator of mankind. And this supreme act of commitment is not of a partial or temporary nature.

Humanity is assumed into the Godhead for all eternity, and what was done in Mary's house at Nazareth when, in response to her loving obedience 'the Word was made Flesh', cannot be undone. The Bridegroom has taken his Church to wife, and those who are incorporated into the Church by baptism are made One Flesh with him for all time. 'My beloved is mine and I am his' sang the writer of the book 'The Song of Solomon'. We belong to Christ and he belongs to us; he has given himself to us freely, eternally, joyfully, in the loving commitment which he made to our common race at the moment of his Incarnation.

Marriage is about commitment and it is about a new beginning, and both these things speak to us of Our Lord and the work of salvation which he has brought about. But also, and on simpler level, marriage is about joy – it is the joyous union of two people, and if that element is missing from a marriage then it can never be that image of Christ's union with his Church which it is meant to be. Properly the union of man and woman in marriage is characterised by joy, and that joy properly flows out from their relationship into the new family of which they will become the centre, and out into the community in which they live. The joy which is meant to characterise marriage again points us to Our Lord Jesus Christ. For he is the source and fountain-head of all joy. It is one of his gifts, communicated to redeemed mankind by his Holy Spirit, and given to us so that we may indeed be formed in the likeness of Christ. Jesus is the very well-spring of our joy, and yet we know that in the course of his incarnate life he entered into every kind of sorrow and suffering as he worked to accomplish our salvation. The incarnate life of Jesus could never be described as comfortable or easy; rather the prophecy of Isaiah that the Messiah would be 'a man of sorrows and acquainted with grief' was abundantly fulfilled. Just so the relationship between husband and wife, whilst it is to be a joyous relationship cannot always be an easy relationship. Marriage is very far from being a soft option for those called to live out this Christian vocation. Times of sorrow, difficulty, and strain, times when great patience and courage and perseverance will be required, are rather to be expected. Maybe the Cross has to be carried in every part and aspect of our living. Yet for Christ the Man of Sorrows the end was resurrection; the sorrows of his passion issued into the supreme joy of that resurrection life which he had won for himself and for the mankind which he had become incarnate to save from eternal death. Christ is risen, and is for ever the cause and centre of our joy. In him alone can we find that which is deeper than mere contentment and richer than mere happiness. By living in him, finding in him our purpose and our peace, we not only share in the joy of the wedding feast at Cana, but anticipate the joy of the marriage supper of the Lamb in heaven.

* * *

Marriage is certainly a new beginning for the two people who enter into it, the beginning of their life together as 'One flesh', as those who God has joined together in a lifelong union. But marriage is of course just one of a great many new beginnings with which Christian people are familiar, the most important one of all being Baptism, in which we begin our new and endless life in Christ, and become new people belonging to a new creation. New beginnings which we experience more frequently include Absolution, when God washes away our faults and failings and in so doing picks us up and allows us to make a new start, a new attempt at living-out what we truly are – citizens of the new Jerusalem. And then whenever we return from the altar after having received the living Christ in Holy Communion we are making a new beginning: we are going out into the world fortified by the Bread of Life, taking with us the Christ who wills and deigns to work for the salvation of his people through our own faltering words and imperfect actions. The Christian knows all about new beginnings, and in doing so he knows about the love of God. For one of the most wonderful ways by which God shows his love for us is in not condemning and rejecting us, but in giving us endless new starts and fresh opportunities to serve him.

Those of us who feel that God is leading us out of our former Anglican allegiance and into what we have come to see as the fullness of Christian truth and life in the Catholic Church, are very much aware that we are standing on the threshold of a new beginning. And we feel, amongst many other things, something of that joyous excitement which is hopefully felt by those who are entering into Christian marriage. Again, as the two people prepare to enter into a new union with one another, a union in which their relationship will be deepened and enhanced, so those of us who are preparing to be received into the Catholic Church are hoping that our future life within it will facilitate the deepening of our relationship with God. And this not perhaps because we feel that the Christian Sacraments as celebrated within the Catholic Church are necessarily more efficacious, or that our life of prayer will somehow be easier and more satisfying within the Roman communion, but rather because we feel that the taking of this step will, if we take it in faith and in loving obedience to the promptings of the Holy Spirit, serve to draw us closer to the Christ who asks us to always do his will. In the past few weeks I've almost taken Abraham as my patron saint; Abraham who was called by God to leave his home and his city, and to go out he knew not where. I've imagined Abraham making just the same excuses that I've tried to make. Abraham telling God what useful work he was doing in Ur, and how he couldn't really be spared. Abraham telling God that he wasn't quite sure that he was hearing God's call correctly and clearly. Abraham wondering whether he'd got the whole thing utterly wrong. Abraham bemoaning the fact that there would never be another croquet lawn or another panelled drawing room like the one at Ur. Abraham finally being honest with God, and saying that he was just scared to leave behind him security and things and people that were familiar, and that made him feel comfortable. But Abraham still being impossible – stretching God's patience to the limit. Then finally, Abraham leaving Ur, trusting God and allowing himself to be moved on to whatever place God had in mind for

him. Abraham making that particular new beginning
through which ultimately he would glorify God and find
salvation.

Making a new beginning and making an act of commitment should properly go together, and certainly those
of us who are being received into the Catholic Church
must see ourselves as doing both things, in just the way
that a bride and bridegroom make a solemn act of commitment as they set out upon their new life together. In
the week or so since I left Wymondham, a number of
kind friends and former parishioners have troubled to
make contact to see whether I have collapsed physically,
mentally, morally and spiritually in the way that some
people had predicted! They have, I think, been pleased
to discover that I am feeling more happy and relaxed
than I've done for some years, but just in case any
encouragement is still needed, several have said 'Well
never mind, you can always come back if you find you've
made a mistake'. Quite apart from the fact that such a
course would hardly be practical, it is also something
which a person in my present situation mustn't even
consider, any more than a person about to commit themselves to another in Christian marriage must think
'well I can always try for a divorce if things don't work
out'. The bride and bridegroom, and likewise the convert, commit themselves 'for better for worse', 'till death
us do part'. 'Haven't you', the accuser may of course say
to me and those in my position 'Haven't you already,
long ago, committed yourself to the Church of England?
And are you not now planning to commit some kind of
spiritual bigamy or adultery or at least a re-marriage
after divorce in becoming a Catholic?' It may be special
pleading, but I don't feel that the analogy quite works.
I do feel that my ultimate commitment must be to God,
and that therefore it is legitimate to move in whatever
direction I feel he is leading me. I shall certainly make
an act of commitment to the Catholic Church at my
reception and I will pray earnestly for grace to always
be true to that commitment: but always my primary
commitment will be and must be to the God who

demands my total allegiance. Further I will not, I hope, be like those young couples who think that the new relationship which they enter into in marriage is going to be roses, roses, all the way. A good marriage is based on solid realism, and in particular in being realistic about your partner's faults and shortcomings! You comit yourself to love them 'warts and all'!

It is good that when a marriage takes place the serious matters of a new beginning and a new and solemn commitment are balanced by the joyous character of the event. In somewhat the same way, I'm looking forward to my reception in a fortnight's time in the expectation that it will be a particularly happy occasion, and indeed today I've been making plans for a party to follow it. I'm looking forward too – and not, I hope unreasonably or unrealistically – to finding a very special happiness in living out the rest of my life as a Catholic. A few months ago one of our church officials and his wife at Wymondham became Catholics, and I asked them some weeks later how they were faring. 'We feel', they said, 'that we've joined a happy church', and I've heard just the same testimony from a number of other recent converts. I'm afraid that for many of us who have lived hitherto as members of the Church of England, our own Church has not in recent years, and even more so in recent months, seemed a particularly happy Church. There have been issues – and most obviously the issue of the Ordination of Women to the priesthood – which have caused an extraordinary amount of division, sadness, and disillusionment, however much the hierarchy may try to pretend that all is well with the Church of England and that everything, in the words of the song, is 'going fine'. Would that it was so, but to many of us it is perfectly clear that it is not. Perhaps the saddest thing of all is to hear devout Anglicans who have practised the Faith all their life, and have been pillars of their local parish churches, say that they are tempted to simply give up their church life, and to know that in some cases this is what is probably going to happen. One of my own reasons for having felt that I must strongly oppose the

Ordination of Women was the fact that it seemed set to cause such hurt and division: how, I asked, could this possibly be from God? Our Lord did indeed say that he had come 'to set father against son and son against father': but that was between the follower of Christ and the one who rejected Christ – not *within* the household of faith itself. Some of my friends in urging me to stay in the Church of England have said 'stay and fight'. But where in this is the joy of living out the Gospel in company and unity with one's fellow believers? Surely to be authentic the Church as the body of Christ must display those principal gifts of the Holy Spirit – Love, Joy, and Peace. For me – and this can only be a personal judgement, with which others are perfectly free to disagree – for me, it is the Catholic Church which most clearly displays these divine gifts of Love, Joy, and Peace, and this makes me more than eager to become part of that Church.

3. *The Mother of Jesus was there*

PEOPLE sometimes point out that if we only had the Fourth Gospel, we wouldn't know the name of Our Lord's Mother. Which is true; St John refers to her only as 'The mother of Jesus'. And yet this omission is clearly not because St John thought Mary insignificant: the reverse is obvious from the fact that the two occasions when she appears in his Gospel are occasions of the highest importance. She stands beneath the Cross on which her Son is dying in the course of his work of redemption, and again she is present at Cana, playing a vital role in facilitating his first miracle, by which he 'revealed his glory and led his disciples to believe in him'. In addition, it is legitimate to see St John as indicating the important role of Mary by choosing to use her title 'Mother of Jesus' in preference to her actual name. It is as if he is saying 'never mind the name, that doesn't matter. Everyone has a name. Concentrate your attention upon the vital and unique role of this woman in bearing the incarnate Word – she is the one in whose womb the Word was made Flesh'.

In those two places where Mary appears in the Fourth Gospel we see her exercising the role of Mother towards Jesus her Son. Her presence at the Cross, supporting and comforting her Son through the long hours of his agony, and seemingly oblivious of her own safety and anguish of spirit – this is a picture of motherhood at its best, exhibiting the deep and sacrificial love of the mother. Then at Cana we see other aspects of motherhood: the mother is one who is free to approach the son on behalf of others because of her special relationship with him – 'They have no wine left', and again like so many mothers (but in her case with complete justification) she has an implicit trust in her son – 'Do whatever he tells you'.

But also at Cana we see Mary exercising a motherly

role towards us, her Son's disciples, and in this already exercising that role of Mother of the Church which Jesus would bestow upon her when from the Cross he gave her to the beloved disciple, as representative of the whole body of disciples in every age. Mary exercises her role as our Mother insofar as she teaches us basic lessons, as a good mother does, about her relationship with God. She teaches us by her example that we too should take our problems and those of other people to Our Lord. 'They have no wine left' Mary prays: 'My brothers and sisters in parts of Africa have no food left': 'I have no love left': 'A man I met earlier today has no faith left' – these are ways in which we might pray, bringing people and problems to the One who is powerful to act, just as Mary our Mother did at Cana. Again, Mary teaches us as Mother how our trust in Jesus must be complete. Even before Jesus had performed any kind of miracle she had complete confidence in his ability to change the course of events – in this case to solve the seemingly insoluble problem of the wine running out. Mary is supremely the woman of faith, the one whose trust and confidence in her Son is absolute. She teaches us at Cana how we must be confident, trustful Christians, and she shames us in that we, unlike her at that stage, have seen so often the mighty acts of Our Lord, and yet our faith still wavers.

It is sometimes said that no family is complete without a Mother, and that the Church, the Family of God, is no exception. In the order of creation the mother has a distinctive and infinitely valuable role to play: she has special gifts to bring to her family, and the sharing of those gifts causes her children to have a special regard for her. She is not – traditionally – considered head of the family, nor does she use her position to dominate it. Rather the good mother is in some respects in the background, facilitating rather than dominating. Maybe it is by defining and examining motherhood in this kind of way that we come to understand the place of Mary in the Christian Church. There is no sense in which she obscures her Son or usurps the place which belongs to him alone. Rather Mary points us towards him, and gently reminds us of all that he is and does. She facilitates and encourages our love and worship not towards herself, but always towards him. In a wholly motherly way she reminds us by her example of our duty towards God, and of the attitude which we should have in situations of stress and difficulty. God has given Mary a vital role in the economy of salvation by inviting her to be the mother of the incarnate Son, the one who gave him that manhood in which he redeemed us. She is, as St John reminds us 'the Mother of Jesus'. She was 'there' at Cana, and we rejoice that she is 'there' in the Church now, supporting her Son's disciples by her prayers and example, and daily encouraging them in their pilgrimage.

* * *

One of the very few 'religious' things which I remember from childhood is asking our elderly Rector why there was so little about Mary in the Bible. I don't know why I should have asked him that – I suspect it was the only thing that I ever did ask him. Maybe it was because of the important place which my own Mother played at home and in my life; she had, I think, a stronger personality than my Father. (I suspect that a pyschologist would see this as a key to some of the things I want to say in this section!) The Rector replied that Mary appears so little in the Gospels so as not to detract attention from Our Lord. A reasonable, safe, Anglican, answer, but betraying no sense of the way in which far from leading us away from Jesus, Mary in fact points us towards him and shows us what it means to be his disciple. There was, of course, no devotion to Mary in our 'middle of the road' Anglican parish church, and I suppose it was only when I encountered Anglo-Catholicism at university that I became aware of her, but then only as one part of the whole Anglo-Catholic package.

As time went by I seem, however, to have been drawn towards her – maybe for psychological reasons – and when during my time at theological college I was also a research student in the University of Oxford, I spent quite a lot of time studying the place of Mary in Anglican theological and devotional literature of the seventeenth-century. This indeed was the subject of the first paper which I had published in a theological journal, and it was in this field too that I made my only significant 'discovery' as a research student – a unique marian devotion in a hitherto unpublished manuscript by Thomas Traherne, which I transcribed and published in the journal *Theology*, with notes and comments. So far, however, my interest in Mary was academic rather than devotional; she played no part in my life of faith and prayer. I accepted her still as part of the 'Catholic package', and because I was very keen to be seen as an Anglo-Catholic I had a picture and later a small statue of her; I also, from the time of being a theological student made occasional pilgrimages to Walsingham, which I came to love deeply as a place. But my actual devotion to Mary still didn't go very far or very deep, and so it remained for a good many years, despite the fact that I had come to a fuller intellectual understanding of the place of Mary in God's scheme of redemption. Not least in this growing understanding was the fact that I had come to understand and accept the dogma of Mary's Assumption. I well remember – with a mixture of shame and amusement – how, when I went to be interviewed for my first curacy, in Newcastle-upon-Tyne, I told the priest with whom I would be working that I felt I must tell him that I did not understand or accept this particular doctrine, and hoped that I wouldn't ever be required to preach on it, as I would find that difficult. The priest very perceptively made no comment, and later it was his own teaching on the Assumption which led me to see that it made perfect sense, and that accepting it was very easy and natural. In those days my attitude was clearly protestant – I was not ready to accept any teaching on authority, but only when I understood it and found it to be reasonable! What, I think, kindled my actual devotion to Mary was not so much being parish priest at Walsingham, which I was from 1977, but more particularly the visit which I made to Lourdes in 1983. Like countless other people who have found themselves there – maybe initially as

visitors rather than pilgrims – I was deeply impressed
(more deeply I think than I realised at the time) by the
remarkable and moving devotion to Mary shown by the
vast crowds. And even more so by the atmosphere in
the domain being charged with a quality of hope and trust
and love and joy which I had never experienced before.
I think it was maybe at Lourdes that I began to have
whatever the marian equivalent is of that 'living faith in
Jesus' of which my evangelical friends speak. And as
always, this led me to have a deeper love for Mary's Son,
for it works like that – to love the Mother is to love the
Son. I have then, I think, taken a further step forward in
the past half dozen years or so, in that I've begun to be
aware of the love and care which Mary has for me as for
all of her Son's disciples. I can't begin to explain it, but
I've come, I suppose to know her as the Mother – the
Mother who was there at Cana and there at the Cross;
the Mother whom Jesus gave to his Church, and who
exercises a truly maternal role within his family.

Like other Anglo-Catholics, I've found it a sadness
that Mary is ignored and misunderstood by so many
Anglicans; that she is, in fact, seen as 'a dead Roman
Catholic' by probably the large majority of Church of
England people. They are happy, it seems, to place her
in stained glass windows and to place her image on ten
thousand Mothers' Union banners, but they refuse her
a place in their minds and in their hearts: in their minds
by failing to recognise her place in God's plan, and in
their hearts by giving her no place in their life of prayer
and devotion. But just as this is a sadness, so it has been
a real difficulty for many of us to find that the honouring
of Mary is not only ignored, but is actually objected to
by a great number of Anglicans. A priest friend used to
say amusingly that Anglicans are 'Wary about Mary',
but one often encounters more than mere wariness. As
an Anglican priest, I've been aware of how the hackles
of many people rise if there is mention of her. In the
average Anglican pulpit it is a delicate subject, and the
priest who wants to avoid hostility has to be extremely
careful about what he says. St John says of Cana that

'The Mother of Jesus was there'; in so many Anglican places of worship Mary is not allowed to be there. Here is an area of universal Christian teaching and practice which is considered alien by a large part of the Church of England; it is not, of course, the only such area. But it is one in which people who are trying to live as Catholics within the Church of England find real difficulty. Theological differences with one's fellow Anglicans are somehow much easier to deal with than devotional or spiritual differences. When you are aware that others are criticising the way in which you conduct your devotional life you feel more exposed, more vulnerable, more easily hurt and offended than in the area of purely doctrinal debate. The devotion which the Catholic-minded person has to Mary is in the same category as his or her love for a human Mother, and to hear one's heavenly Mother defamed or even ignored causes just the same pain and offence which would be very natural in regard to one's own human mother.

When I become a Catholic in a few days time I'm looking forward to being part of a Church where the Mother of Jesus is most certainly 'there', and there in the sense that she is recognised and welcomed. There, teaching, loving, and caring for her spiritual children, just as she did at Cana, and pointing them always towards her divine Son. And more especially I'm looking forward to being where Mary is in a right sense, 'taken for granted'. A place where Mary is not only present, but where her presence is seen as perfectly normal; where there is a complete naturalness about devotion to her, and where she is given her proper place in the lives of the brothers and sisters of her Son. I'm looking forward to all this because I believe it is in accordance with God's will.

4. *Jesus and His Disciples were Guests also*

THE INCIDENT which St John describes is thronged with people, which I suppose is how we would expect it to be on the occasion of a village wedding. Besides the Bride and Bridegroom there are the steward, the servants, Mary, Jesus and his disciples, and then all the friends, relations, and villagers. It is a crowded scene, a gathering of people for what is rightly a communal event. A marriage has both a private and a public aspect; certainly the latter, for it is an event which affects society in that through the marriage a new unit is created in society.

Human beings are, we are reminded, social animals. God has made them not to live and work in isolation, but to live and work as part of a whole. And this is as true of mankind in its religious aspect as in its secular aspect. Our salvation requires that we be incorporated into Christ; in accordance with God's plan we must be joined to the Christ who has died and who is risen, so that we may be sharers in his new and endless life. St Paul likens this to the process of grafting; we are grafted into Christ so that his life flows into us and causes us to be alive in him. Again St Paul says that it is like becoming limbs, arms and legs, of a human body in which Christ is the head. And this grafting, this incorporation into Christ comes about in the Sacrament of Baptism, the very simple way which God has chosen as the means, the occasion, by which we become one with Christ, joined to him, sharers in the life with which he rose from the dead. Now if we become one with Christ in baptism, then we obviously and necessarily become one with all those other people who have been incorporated into him; we become part of his body, that is part of the sum of all those countless other people with whom he has shared his risen life. We become in fact members of his Church, which consists of all those who have been joined to him sacramentally in baptism. We are not the only person who is sharing his endless life: rather we are part of a great company 'which no man can number', part of a throng stretching around the world and across the centuries, part of the Church of God, which exists on earth and in heaven. So there is, in one sense, no such thing as individual salvation; rather we are saved as part of the whole, as limbs of the one body. As Christians we live and experience salvation within the divine society of the Church, enjoying a common life with our fellow Christians even as we share with them a common hope and a common purpose.

Being the Church then, being part of that divine society which Our Lord founded and which has its essential and fundamental oneness because He, the Christ, is the heart, the centre, the life-giver, of his mystical body – this living as members of the Church, the body of Christ, is no peripheral matter as regards the living out of our vocation as Christian people. Rather being the Church, living as members of the Church is a basic part of our response to God's plan for us and to the offer of eternal life which he makes to us. We come as one people, the people of God, to one table, to be nourished with the one Bread of Life. We hold, live by, and proclaim, the one Faith, the truth entrusted by the one Lord to his body, his bride the Church. At baptism we were born into the community of the Church just as those villagers at Cana had been born into a local community and shared fully in its life, in its joys and in its sorrows, supporting one another and encouraging one another. Together in times of crisis; sometimes locked in disputes; getting on better with some members of the community than others; aware that different members of that community had certain outstanding gifts and abilities, and that others made rather less of a contribution to the common life. But accepting one another, aware that their fortunes and destinies were ultimately entwined; accepting each other as part of a particular society, having, at the end of the day, an overriding common interest.

In the scene at Cana, see how there is an 'earthly'

focus and also a 'divine' focus. The Bride and Bridegroom clearly form the 'earthly' focus: it is their day, it
is their union which is being celebrated, and in this
respect they are quite rightly at the centre of the stage.
But then there is another focus, a 'divine' focus, and this
is obviously Jesus himself. He is the dominating figure,
the one who has the power to order events and to turn
a crisis into a triumph. Perhaps it is not too fanciful to
suggest that there is some parallel to this within the life
of the Church. Christ is the 'divine' focus: it is his
Church, his body. The body is alive with his life, and
lives in obedience to him. He truly is Lord of the Church,
and every member of it is his servant, his disciple. And
yet the Christ gave authority to the earthly leadership
of his Church. He gave Peter the keys of the kingdom;
authority to absolve in his name and to withhold absolution; authority to teach in his name – 'Feed my sheep'.
So that there is a proper sense in which Peter and his
successor forms an 'earthly' focus in the Church, a focus
willed and instituted by Christ the Head of the Church,
and always borne in obedience to him. A God-given focus
which is necessary for the well-being of the Church, being
a valuable and necessary means of its ensuring and
safeguarding the unity of its teaching and purpose.

Whilst the incident at Cana presents us first and
foremost with a picture of community, of wholeness, of
mankind living in society in just the way in which God
intended man and women to live, there are certainly
moments of intimacy in the picture, moments of individual encounter in this scene which St John describes.
The Mother speaks privately with the Son, explaining
the problem which has arisen, and implicitly asking him
to resolve it; the steward speaks privately to the bridegroom, questioning him about the good wine; and Jesus
it seems acts privately in performing the miracle, since
St John suggests that only the servants knew the origin
of the wine which so impressed the steward. Here
perhaps we are reminded that whilst the community is
primary – we live and are saved first and foremost as
members of the Body, as part of the divine society of the

Church – yet still the individual is never submerged in that community so as to become indistinct and insignificant. For whilst God saves us as part of the whole, he has made us and he knows us and loves us as individuals. The very fact that each one of us is so different, with different gifts and abilities and even with a different appearance, testifies to this. We are not cogs or numbers, rather we are sons and daughters, each of us known and of infinite worth to our heavenly Father. Jesus assured us of this in his parables of the lost sheep and the lost coin, and in the care and interest which he had for even unattractive individuals such as Bartimaeus and Zacchaeus. Each of us is called to have an individual relationship with God, which is conducted and deepened most obviously within our own individual life of private prayer when, in accordance with Our Lord's teaching and practice we go into a private place and put ourselves in the presence of God.

There must be a balance between the communal and the private in our religion, based upon the fact that whilst the first is primary, the second is necessary. Any society – whether human or claiming to be divine – in which the individual is crushed, ignored, considered unimportant, can never be in accordance with the will of God who made us and loves us as individuals. Such a society will itself be inhuman and doomed to failure and ultimately to extinction. But similarly a Church which sits light to its oneness, and whose members feel themselves to be first and foremost individuals, free to pick and choose what they believe, and not bound by the wisdom of the whole and by properly – divinely – instituted authority within the whole – this too cannot be truly the Church, the single body, which Our Lord came to found. We are individuals, but we are not free to act unilaterally. We are under authority to Christ: to him, and not first and foremost to our own interpretation of Christ's teaching, but rather to the wisdom of the whole body of which we are merely individual members. There is a certain and necessary humility in accepting this. We are not as individuals God, nor infallible interpreters of God, and we

need to recognise that the whole body of Christ guided,
directed and enlighted by the Holy Spirit down the ages
is rather more likely to have got it right than we are as
individual members of the body!

*   *   *

I think it is probably true to say that in the last few
decades there has been a growth in understanding, both
inside and outside the Catholic Church, regarding the
nature and the importance of the Church as the body
of Christ, the People of God, and further that in this
development the whole feeling as well as the documents
of the Second Vatican Council have played a vital role.
Christians in the Protestant as well as in the Catholic
tradition have been encouraged to see themselves as
being first and foremost part of the whole rather than
isolated individuals, and this development in Christian
thinking – a rediscovery rather than any kind of completely new insight – has led to a certain amount of
questioning concerning both how the Church ought to
be and the part that each one of us is called to fulfil
within it.

In particular, many of us within the Anglican Church
have been led to question whether or not we are justified
in remaining outside the mainstream of western
Christendom; whether it is right for us to continue to be
'protestants', and what exactly it is that we are protesting
about. And further, whether the nature of our protest is
such that it makes it right and reasonable for us to continue in separation from the Catholic Church? And this
I believe is a question which is raised not least by the
fact that the Roman Church has changed very considerably in the past few decades. Some of the causes of our
original 'protest' in the sixteenth century are now totally
extinct: so are we now protesting just for the sake of it?
Is the wholeness, the full organic unity of the Church
being sacrificed in fact to no good purpose? I think these
questions have been highlighted for some of us by our
experiences, very common experiences these days, of
staying on holiday in such countries as France, Italy,
Spain, and of worshipping with our fellow Christians

there. Maybe it has saddened us and disturbed us that we are not in communion with them, and that although they are invariably most hospitable in allowing us to receive the Sacrament at their altars, nevertheless we know full well that this is not in accordance with the discipline of the Catholic Church. Last Autumn I went with a party from Wymondham Abbey to Normandy, and one of our purposes was to visit the tiny village in the diocese of Coutances from which the founder of the Abbey had originated nine hundred years ago. The hospitality which the villagers offered us, both in their parish church and in the village hall afterwards was unforgettable; just the kind of warm hospitality which St Paul urges Christian people to extend to one another. But the fact remained that although one in Christ through our common baptism, we were not in ecclesial terms in communion with each other. And the fault of this, I believed, was on our side. We were the 'protestants', part of a break away from the integrity of Catholic Christendom. Was our stand and our status still justified in post Vatican II days? Or were we, are we, guilty of perpetuating division within what should be the one, whole, unified, Church – the seamless robe, the unbroken body of Christ?

In recent months I've come to ask myself these questions in a more pressing way, and to feel that I ought to act in accordance with whatever answers seemed to be given me. And further, I find that I've come – for want of a more theological description – to see the sense of the papacy as well as the importance of the unity of the Church. Unlike some of my fellow Anglo-Catholics, the papacy as an institution has never moved nor impressed me very much; I've certainly never been any kind of papalist. Well, it is always said that you need to be either very clever or very unintelligent to be an Anglo-Papalist, and I suppose I'm not really either. Yet it has always stuck in my mind that when reading the collected works of King James I in the course of my seventeenth-century studies, I came upon a passage in which he said that a reformed papacy should be accepted as according with the will of God for his Church, and in the realm of ideas

King James was certainly no fool . . . Be that as it may,
I've come to believe firmly that a strong central authority
within the Church, a centre of unity, but more than that
a centre of truth, is necessary to its well being, and is an
easily understandable and very reasonable part of God's
plan for his Church. Perhaps this has been made particularly clear by comparison with the Church of England,
which doesn't possess the kind of focus of authority and
hence of unity which the papacy provides for the Catholic
Church. To some of us, the decision of the General Synod
of the Church of England to proceed unilaterally with the
Ordination of Women represents amongst other things
the fact that a Church without such a strong central teaching authority can easily be blown hither and thither – some
would say derailed – by the force of fashionable move-
ments in secular culture, in this particular case secular
feminism. Peter, the Rock, gives the Catholic Church just
that firm foundation which allows the Church to hold firm
in times of perplexity and dispute.

Last Autumn my old Anglican theological college
offered a Retreat for former students, and I was very
keen to go, not least because the retreat was to be conducted by a well-known theologian for whom I have a great
respect. Sadly things don't always turn out as one
expects, and I discovered that this was no ordinary
retreat. Instead of spiritual addresses, designed to deepen
and stimulate our spiritual life, I and my fellow
retreatants were given a series of lectures on the catholicity of the Church of England, designed to convince us
that there was no reason why we should find it unsatisfactory and leave it! Fascinating and excellent though
these lectures were, they were not at all what we were
expecting. In one of them the Conductor, a former Canon
of Christ Church, Oxford, reminded us of how Dr Samuel
Johnson had remarked that it was a 'great thing' to dine
with the Canons of Christ Church. The Conductor suggested that likewise it was a 'great thing' to be in communion with the bishop of Rome, but far from being a
necessary thing. I'm afraid that the good conductor's
words had quite the opposite effect on me to that which

was intended. It was a moment of revelation. I knew instinctively that being in communion with the successor of Peter was not at all analogous with dining with the Canons of Christ Church, and I saw very clearly which of these two things genuinely mattered!

I've come to believe that the papacy makes a great deal of sense, and likewise that the dogma of Papal Infallibility makes sense too. This dogma seems to present great problems to many Anglicans, often, dare I say, because they suppose that it operates much more widely and includes far more things than it actually does. It applies, of course, only when the Pope is defining doctrine, which is a fairly rare occurrence. Again it is a safeguard for the integrity of revealed truth, and is to be seen primarily in this way. To me for one, it seems perfectly reasonable and wholly in line with Our Lord's promise to Peter, that when the head of the Church here on earth – the 'earthly focus' – proclaims Christian teaching in the most solemn manner possible, that he will indeed be proclaiming what is true, and not misleading or deceiving the sheep whom Christ has charged Peter to feed. And further I believe that just as the Holy Spirit will guide the bishop of Rome on these particular occasions, so too it is the Holy Spirit who has guided the Church down the centuries to become centred, in the interests of unity and truth, upon the See of Rome.

Then just as I have come to see the importance of being part of the one universal Church, part of the one community of the faithful, so too I have come to see more clearly the unsatisfactory nature of relying on individual judgement and interpretation rather than upon the teaching and wisdom of the whole Church. It is of course of the very essence of Protestantism – at least of the kind of liberal protestantism which is so widespread in the Church of England at present – to allow the individual to decide for him or her self what is right and true in matters of faith and morality. To act as if there was no objective truth, nothing revealed, nothing to be accepted on authority. This leads to a strange kind of à la carte religion, where each person takes or leaves the individual teachings of the Church just as they please. Rather like a kind of spiritual buffet, in which you move along taking a little of whatever pleases your fancy. This cannot be right in a revealed religion such as Christianity, where it has always been held that truth has been given and is therefore objective and to be received with faith. Given not piecemeal to individuals, but given to the whole Church, to be understood, accepted, guarded and taught by the whole Church. And here, of course, we have to practise a kind of humility which I feel I've also come to understand. I recognise and accept that I can't enter the Catholic Church saying that whilst I accept the main body of its teaching there is nevertheless this, and this, and this dogma which I can't agree to. To say that, is to say that I, John Barnes, know better than the Church down the ages; that I know better than my fellow members within the body of Christ; that I know better than the successor of Peter; that my own tin-pot judgement and understanding is superior to that of the universal Church. This would be preposterous, and I'd be the biggest fool in Christendom if I held to that.

So where does this leave individuality, the individuality which God has given each one of us, and which is represented at Cana by the moments of intimacy and of individual encounter? Well those moments are of course contained within the framework of the community gathered to celebrate the marriage. And perhaps this suggests how our individuality is to flourish, flower, find itself, express itself, within that organisational and intellectual framework with which the Catholic Church provides its members. At Wymondham the garden surrounding the Vicarage is walled, and within the walls there is an abundance of vegetation (weeds as well as flowers I'm afraid!) and freedom for plants and shrubs of all kinds to grow and develop and come to maturity. The walls are no negative kind of constraint, and indeed some plants are very dependent upon those walls for their support and well-being. In rather the same way I believe that the framework for living and believing which the Catholic Church provides for her members by means of her definitive teaching is to be seen in a positive way, as being necessary for our spiritual health and development. Those very boundaries and constraints are aids rather than hindrances to our growth in grace and holiness, and allow us as individuals not to be suppressed and subdued, but rather to come to maturity within the Body of Christ.

5. *The Wine Gave Out*

St John's bald statement of the situation 'the wine gave out' is well-suited to describe this moment of crisis at the wedding. It was what in most cultures and generations would be considered a disaster; certainly in England today just as in first century Palestine a wedding at which the wine ran out would be considered 'a poor do'. Perhaps there would be recriminations. Had the family been too mean to lay in sufficient supplies, were they trying to stage the wedding on the cheap? Or had something been going on behind the scenes – had those servants or the steward made away with some of the wine prepared for the occasion? Or had some of the guests simply been greedy, and drunk far more than their fair share? Recriminations perhaps on the part of some, but as regards the bride and bridegroom, just a terrible disappointment and embarrassment. This was meant to be their special day, a once and for all occasion, something to remember. Remember it they would, as would all the guests: the wedding at which the wine ran out, the one where the guests went home thirsty and grumbling. The hearts of the bride and bridegroom must have been heavy indeed, and I like to think that it was an understanding of how this young couple felt which prompted Our Lord to perform his first miracle: not a miracle prompted by some plague or famine, some illness or death, but simply by the unhappiness of a young couple on their wedding day, when the wine ran out at the reception.

It was a crisis, the wine failing, and a crisis which humanly speaking it seemed impossible to resolve. For there appeared to be nothing that anyone could do: a disaster – very minor in the face of eternity, but miserable for those at its centre – which simply had to be endured. No one could have imagined that there would or could be any way out of the situation except of course Mary the woman of faith. Mary alone looked in the right direction for an answer to the problem – she knew that Jesus could make everything come right and transform a situation of crisis into one of wonder and delight, and so she turned to him with a simple statement of what had gone wrong 'they have no wine left'.

We thought earlier of how this first of the Signs which Our Lord performed points forward to the last and greatest of the Signs, the resurrection of Jesus. It does so not least in that here at Cana there is a situation of a crisis to which there seems to be no possible solution. The supplies of wine were dead just as the crucified body of Jesus was dead on Good Friday, and in both cases that seemed to be an end to the matter. The springs were dry. But then in both cases the unimaginable happened and the seemingly intractable crisis was resolved. New wine, new life, and in both situations a manifestation of the glory of the incarnate Christ. But this only happening as a result of a crisis which was real and complete. The wine didn't nearly run out, like the widow's oil and meal in the Old Testament. And Jesus didn't nearly die, as King Hezekiah nearly died, when he was crucified. Only when things were utterly hopeless was the divine power displayed; the crisis had to be absolute before the answer was given.

*   *   *

I said above that the crisis of the wine running out during the marriage at Cana was a very minor crisis in the sight of eternity. So too perhaps in the sight of eternity was that crisis which overtook some of us when the General Synod of the Church of England passed the legislation which opened up the way for the ordination of women to the priesthood on November 11th 1992, but it was none the less real. To many, of course, this was no crisis at all. To many in fact it was an answer to prayer, and to even more people it was a perfectly reasonable, sensible, and completely unremarkable thing to have happened. I suppose it might be asked here and now whether or not the crisis which some of us believed there to be over the Ordination of Women was not in reality, 'much

ado about nothing' – especially when we think of terrible
world crises involving the lives, rights, and welfare of
people: crises such as the recent massacres in Rwanda,
the atrocities committed in Bosnia, and the starvation in
various parts of the Sudan. Compared with these things
can we really talk about a 'crisis' over the Ordination of
Women? It's tempting I suppose to say no, but I don't
think it would be right to do so. For matters of truth and
conscience, matters concerning God's revelation and our
response to it, do in fact matter. Just as matters of justice
and human welfare matter too. It is not a case of 'either/
or', and the one kind of crisis mustn't be allowed to make
the other seem irrelevant. I say without apology that for
many the events of November 11th 1992 were a crisis –
as real and as distressing a crisis as the one which arose
for the bride and bridegroom at Cana, when the wine
ran out at their marriage feast.

At the time when the vote was taken on the Priests
(Ordination of Women) Measure I had been a member
of the General Synod for seven years. I decided to stand
in the 1985 elections principally so that I could oppose
the above Measure which, at that time, seemed likely to
be decided during the life of 1985–1990 Synod. When
this didn't happen, I stood again in 1990, and for just
the same purpose. Standing for the Synod for the primary
purpose of opposing a particular measure may seem
horribly negative. I would say two things in my defence.
First, that I felt this particular issue to be so important
to the well-being, credibility, and integrity of the Church
of England that I thought such a course of action justified. I believed that if this measure was passed, there
would be anarchy in the church and equally that the
Church of England would be betraying its essential
principles and its very nature. And then second, that
although I became a member of the Synod for this one
purpose, I nevertheless tried to play a full part in its life.
I attended every group of sessions during the seven years,
and sat for hours in the debating chamber, (more often
than not hot, uncomfortable, and bored stiff,) and on the
two occasions when I was called to speak – being called

is far from easy, and for most members only happens very occasionally – I spoke on subjects other than the Ordination of Women – on worship, and working with children.

Why was it that I felt so strongly about the ordination of women as priests? Fundamentally because I felt far from convinced that this innovation was in accordance with God's will for his Church. Indeed I felt, and I continue to feel, that there are factors which suggest otherwise. I feel the fact that Jesus called only male apostles is relevant. There were certainly women amongst the people who followed Jesus, but none of them was included in the twelve. People say that women apostles would not have been acceptable at that time, but surely in other areas Jesus didn't seem to be afraid of innovation, and of flouting convention? And then the fact that when the three-fold ministry began to emerge in the first and second centuries it remained male seems to be relevant. Again people say that women priests would not have been acceptable in the Jewish world. But within a relatively short time the Church had moved out of a Jewish milieu into a world where women priests were perfectly normal and acceptable – nevertheless, the Christian priesthood remained male. Might this not have been because God meant it to be so? Then all down the centuries this continued to be the case: a male priesthood in a Church which, we believe, continued to be guided by the Holy Spirit. Women saints, women abbesses, women as spiritual guides, but never women as priests. Was God's will really being frustrated all that time? Or had he genuinely got a 'U' turn up his sleeve, waiting for 1992?

Then there are other factors too which suggest that women priests are not perhaps part of God's plan. The fact that the second person of the Holy Trinity took male humanity at the incarnation seems to make it appropriate that the priest who represents him at the Altar should be male. All Christians of course are called to represent Christ, indeed to be other Christs. And yet there is a very particular way in which the priest – unworthy though he is – represents Christ, not least liturgically. Again, I felt that the fact that the ordination of women would damage the Church of England's ecumenical relationships, both with Rome and with Constantinople (something which has now happened) was very relevant. We believed that the advances in ecumenism, represented for example by the ARCIC agreements, were the work of the Holy Spirit: so how could something which would cause a setback on this front also come from God? And then finally, it seemed to be a fact that the whole question had arisen in the wake of militant feminism; might it be that the move to ordain women to the priesthood had its origin in a secular movement rather than in a genuine leading of the Holy Spirit? All these considerations made me think – rightly or wrongly – that the proposed move might well not be in accordance with God's will, and that the only way of discovering God's will in the matter was to wait and see if a major part of the whole people of God throughout Christendom felt that this was where the Church was being led, a position which has manifestly not been reached at the present time and which may or may not emerge in the future.

I found the year or so before the Synod vote a considerable strain, as did so many other people. A dark shadow seemed to be hanging over the Church. During that time the diocesan synods voted on the question, and before that the various Deanery Synods within each diocese. Each Deanery Synod debated the matter before taking its vote, and as a member of the General Synod I was asked to put the case against the Measure on a number of occasions. At each Deanery synod meeting I elaborated on the points which I've made above, trying to emphasise that I was no misogynist, and that the matter we were debating was not to do with women's rights but with God's will. I was at pains to explain that to suggest that women may not be called to the priesthood was not to imply that they are in any way inferior to men, any more than to say that an arm is inferior to a leg simply because it doesn't have the same function. I also wanted to make it clear that I was not what has come to be

called an 'impossibilist': I don't think we can say categ-
orically that God does not intend that there should ever
be women priests, i.e. that it is impossible for a woman
to be priest: rather we simply don't know. And that in
matters concerned with salvation – and through celebrat-
ing the Sacraments the priest is involved with the process
of salvation – it simply won't do not to know for sure
whether someone is truly a priest or not. But however
clearly and well I tried to put my case, I was aware time
after time that I was making little headway. The people,
I felt, were not prepared to think theologically. They
asked why, if we could have a woman doctor, couldn't
we have a woman priest? And they said that some of the
women deacons they'd already met were very nice . . .
It tended to be on that level, and was deeply depressing.
As in the final General Synod debate. I felt that we the
opponents had won the argument but lost the debate.
Also I much disliked being in the role of opponent to
what was proposed: I think I'm a positive person by
nature, and to appear to be negative and prejudiced was
not in itself a pleasant experience.

And then of course November came. Many of my
fellow Anglo-Catholics seemed complacent, and said that
the Measure would never get through. I hoped they were
right, but felt sure that it could go either way, and
thought those who said there was no need to worry were
being unrealistic. Certainly everyone agreed that it
would be a close-run thing, as indeed it was. Those who
watched the debate on television will remember how
tense those hours were, and as a member with very strong
feelings on the matter I was gripping my seat, hoping
against hope that each speaker would sway the Synod
towards rejecting the Measure. I left straight after the
vote was announced – my final exit from Church House
and the General Synod – to find a vast crowd of women-
priest enthusiasts outside the building, singing and
shouting and cheering, a vivid contrast with some of the
women from the Catholic Group in Synod whom I'd seen
weeping in the corridors inside. It made one feel an odd
kind of numb hopeless anger, and as I tried to push my

way through the press of triumphant women on the steps I felt an urge to roughly push them down onto the pavement below. I'm ashamed of those feelings now.

When I got back to the parish, to Wymondham, the impact of what had happened in London began to sink in. Next morning at 7.30 a.m. I was at Morning Prayer as usual, but felt utterly unable to take part in the Eucharist which followed. Rather unfairly I left it to my two curates – who were also distressed – and went home. I asked them both to come round for a drink before Evening Prayer, and they arrived together, convinced that I wanted to tell them that I had resigned the living and was leaving the Church of England immediately. In fact I had written to the bishop in the course of the day, but had only asked him to accept my resignation from the General Synod and from the Chairmanship of the Diocesan Advisory Committee – I just wanted to see my colleagues so that we could discuss the situation together and hear their views. I had told the bishop – in a letter which was not quite so cool and courteous as I could have wished in retrospect – that I could no longer belong to a provincial synod which behaved as if it was a general council (i.e. in taking unilaterally a decision which could only properly be taken by the whole of Christendom), and that I wished to resign from the diocesan committee I looked after as I needed time to consider my future. I received a kind and courteous reply.

In the meditation on the crisis at Cana with which this section began, I said that when the wine ran out all seemed lost – there seemed to be no obvious or available solution, just disaster, a crisis that would remain unresolved. And further, how it was this seemingly hopeless situation which allowed Jesus to act, to do that unexpected and unimagined thing which would bring light out of darkness and be nothing less than a manifestation of his glory. Well, I cannot claim that the crisis which I've described above exactly parallels the crisis at Cana. In both situations there was certainly distress and anxiety and whatever else we associate with the experience of crisis. But whilst at Cana there was no obvious way out, no solution to the problem of the empty wine jars, in 1992 many of us began to realise as the dust settled that there was in fact a way forward – a way which I suppose had been at the back of our minds but which we knew we must now seriously consider. It was almost as if our spiritual mother had left us, but there was nevertheless an aunt who would maybe take us in . . . And so I for one began to look in the direction of the Catholic Church. It was not quite a darkness into light, death into life, experience like the one at Cana, a sudden and unexpected intervention by the Christ, but I was nevertheless aware that the One who transforms and resolves situations was acting, and that in however small a way I was being made aware of his power and his glory.

6. *Do Whatever He Tells You*

'Do whatever he tells you': with these simple words Mary tells the servants at the marriage that they must do two things. First, that they must be attentive. That they must listen to Jesus, and hear what he is saying. Then second, that they must be ready, without delay or equivocation, to do exactly what he commands. Mary repeats her words at Cana to all of her Son's disciples, in every age and place. We need to hear them as much as the servants did, for we too are servants, servants of Mary's Son. It is fundamental to being good, faithful, efficient, profitable servants that we listen – we will be of little use to our Master unless we do. All too often, however, we are over-confident servants, sometimes forgetting that we are servants at all. We pursue our own course, we think we know best and that it is unnecessary for us to be constantly attentive to God, straining to listen so that we may discover just what it is that he wants us to do. How the kingdom of God would have advanced, and how it could be advanced now, if only the servants in God's household would listen to him carefully and constantly, and so have a true knowledge of his will.

The Mother teaches us, and so too do the servants at Cana. They teach us by the fact that they did what Mary said – they did in fact choose to listen to Jesus and then to do what he told them. In this we are reminded of how we as disciples are not called to be robots or automatons, but rather to work in free co-operation with the will of God. God has given us freedom of will, freedom to choose what we will do and be. It is one of his greatest gifts to us, and it bestows upon us an extraordinary worth and dignity. It enables us to choose God, to turn to him with trust and love, and to work in partnership with him. It makes us able to say Yes to God, as Mary herself said Yes to God at the Annunciation. If the servants at Cana had ignored Mary's charge to them, supposing that they were too busy to listen to the directions given by Jesus, and again if they had been too proud to listen to him and obey him, then maybe the miracle would not have taken place, and the glory of Jesus would have remained undisclosed on that occasion. The servants had a vital part to play, and so too have we. Unless we look and listen, unless we in our own situation 'do whatever he tells us', then God's work will remain undone and his glory will remain unrevealed.

Perhaps most of us find in the spiritual life that we need constantly to be reminding ourselves of fundamental truths; that again and again we need to attend to the obvious rather than to the over-sophisticated and the novel, which can sometimes be little more than distractions. We need to remind ourselves of the simple facts that God is present with us wherever we are; that he loves us, and that he loves the neighbour whom we find unlovable. That he is in charge, and able to bring light out of darkness, and order out of the chaos in our lives. That we can trust him, and know that ultimately the victory is his. We also need to remind ourselves of the essentials of discipleship: listening, attending, and being ready straightaway to do what he tells us.

*   *   *

Listening, being attentive. Having the humility to seek God's will and the wisdom to do it. In the second part of the last chapter, I tried to describe the crisis which I and many others experienced over the decision of the General Synod to permit the ordination of women to the priesthood. I said why I felt so strongly that this decision was wrong – wrong at least at the time when it was taken, because to my mind the will of God in this matter was far from clear. But the majority of Anglicans and apparently not a few Roman Catholics thought that the decision taken by the Synod was right, and applauded it. You may be one of those people, and if so you probably read the last chapter with a feeling of exasperation. How, you maybe asked, could I be so blind and prejudiced; how could I be swayed by arguments

which seem so weak and inconclusive? And above all,
how could I have been so deaf, so inattentive, to the
voice of God as, in answer to much prayer, he let his
will be known through the sizable majority in the Synod
which voted for the Measure? And if you felt exasperated
when reading what I wrote in the previous chapter, then
you maybe feel disgusted when you find that in this chapter I have had the affrontery to go on to write about
listening to God and doing what he says.

I hope fervently that I wasn't being blind, deaf, and
ultimately disobedient to the will of God. Certainly in
the course of the 'campaign' which preceded the vote I
tried to keep reminding myself and others that the one
thing which mattered was the discovery of God's will.
Simply because it is his Church, not ours, and we are
servants, not masters, in the household of God. Well,
why couldn't I accept that God had revealed his will
through the Synod's vote? Essentially because I could
not accept the Synod as an authority which could be
relied upon in matters of doctrine, and still less as any
kind of ultimate authority. I saw myself, as the Anglican
divines of the seventeenth-century whose works I'd
studied had seen themselves, as being first and foremost
part of something larger than the Church of England:
part of the One, Holy, Catholic and Apostolic Church
of which the Anglican Communion is only one relatively
small part. And part in such a way that it does not belong
to the Church of England to innovate in matters of order
and doctrine; this, the Church of England has always
and rightly been held in the past, can only be done by
the whole Church. People often quote the words of
Archbishop Geoffrey Fisher – words especially powerful
insofar as he was not himself an Anglo-Catholic – that
the Church of England has no doctrine of her own, but
only what has been held universally and from the beginning by the whole Church Catholic and Apostolic. However in the Priests (Ordination of Women) Measure – to
give it its correct title – the Church of England was, for
the first time, forging a doctrine which was its own, a
teaching that was totally unknown to the rest of Catholic

Christendom. It was this that I was referring to in the last chapter when I spoke of the Church of England losing its integrity, and not being true to its own principles. This too is what was meant when people spoke of the Church of England having forfeited its claim to be considered a legitimate part of the One, Holy, Catholic and Apostolic Church in that it had begun creating its own teaching, independently and indeed in defiance of the main body of the Church.

But did God speak through the General Synod, and did I fail to listen to him? In my studies in seventeenth-century Anglican thought (and the writings of that period are usually accepted as representing Anglican thought at its best – a sort of 'patristic period' of Anglicanism) I had become well acquainted with the characteristic Anglican theological method for discovering the truth, namely that three-fold appeal to Scripture, Tradition, and Reason which was first worked-out in the late sixteenth-century by the man who was arguably the greatest Anglican teacher, Richard Hooker. Was it God's will that women should be ordained to the priesthood? For me as an Anglican the answer to that question was not to be found in blind obedience to the two-thirds majority of the General Synod of the Church of England, but by following the traditional Anglican three-fold appeal. Following this appeal, I believed that I had found a negative answer, as I suggested in the last chapter. I felt that whilst the Scriptures give no definitive answer, the fact that those called to be apostles were all male was relevant and suggestive; that the fact of the priesthood being male all down the centuries, universally, was also suggestive in view of the fact that the Holy Spirit has, in accordance with Our Lord's promise, been guiding the Church; and also on the grounds of Reason it seemed unlikely that God was asking for female priests when such a move would be divisive and impede rather than promote the unity and the mission of the Church. Thus as a believer in the rightness of the traditional Anglican way of discovering God's truth and God's will, as well as a member of the universal rather than just the local

Church, I did not feel that God had necessarily spoken through the majority vote of the Synod. I believed it right to seek the truth and hopefully to listen to God's voice, in other more venerable and respected quarters.

'Do whatever he tells you.' Have I in the near two-year period since the vote been listening to God, in planning to leave the Church of England and to leave the parish which, I believe, God put into my charge five years ago when he sent me there as parish priest? And when I am received into the Catholic Church in a week's time, will that truly be an act of obedience – will I be like the servants at Cana who listened to Jesus and then did what he told them? I hope so and I believe so. Like, I suspect, many of my fellow Christians I feel ashamed that I don't give more time to private prayer. I know how much it matters, and this not least because it is often in private prayer that God tells us what he wants us to do. But I have prayed during these months, and on one occasion in particular I felt that God was speaking to me. Earlier this year when I was saying my prayers in Wymondham Abbey one morning I said to God rather desperately about the future 'If only I knew what to do', meaning, I hope 'if only, I knew for certain what you want me to do'. Very clearly I heard inside myself a voice saying quietly but firmly 'John you do know what to do'. I still feel that this was a confirmation of the course which I had then embarked upon, the process of becoming a Catholic. I think that God in his infinite mercy has told me what to do, and now I pray for grace to follow it through.

7. *There were Six Stone Water-jars . . . Each Held from Twenty to Thirty Gallons*

SURELY any reader of St John's account of the incident at Cana must be struck by the sheer quantity of water which was transformed into wine. Perhaps there is some kind of mystical significance in the numbers which St John provides. Or maybe he simply wants his readers to realise that Jesus provided not just a few extra bottles or jugs, but rather a great sea of wine – around one hundred and eighty gallons of it. For the very quantity of the wine serves to speak of the divine generosity, and this is perhaps more important than the quantity being merely a reminder of the scale on which God works. Yes, the scale does serve to remind us that the Christ who performed this miracle is the divine Word 'through whom all things come to be': the Word who creates the vastness of space and the immensity of time. But more than that it reminds us that our God is a generous God, whose love matches the scale of his working.

The same largeness of working that is seen in the making of around one hundred and eighty gallons of wine at Cana is seen too in that later miracle, recorded in chapter six of the Fourth Gospel, when Jesus fed a vast crowd of people on the hillside. Again St John wants us to know the numbers, five thousand people fed and twelve baskets of scraps collected up afterwards, just so that we may contemplate that generosity which characterises the working of God. Together, of course, these two miracles – the one at Cana concerning wine and the one on the hillside concerning bread – point us forward to the great and abiding miracle whereby the Christ feeds the souls of his people in the Eucharist. Here, as

Christians are fed at a hundred thousand altars day by
day and century after century, is a constant manifestation
of that abundant generosity which marks the whole of
God's dealing with his people.

But see how alongside the broad and lavish gesture of
providing such a large quantity of wine, a gesture which
speaks of the scale and generosity of God's working, there
is by contrast the delicate and intimate understanding
of the feelings of the two young people. To some the
disappointment and embarrassment of this obscure bride
and bridegroom on their wedding day might seem utterly
unimportant and insignificant – not worth noticing, not
deserving of consideration. But as we've thought already,
it was this very thing, this seemingly small thing, which
prompted the first of Our Lord's miracles. We find that
the largeness of God's working is matched by the largeness of his love. And that the fact that he works on a
scale which amazes us by its size does not mean that
he is unmindful of what is usually counted small and
unimportant.

*   *   *

As I've struggled with the matter of what I ought to do
in the new situation which has arisen in the Church of
England, I've repeatedly and I think properly asked the
question 'Does it matter?'. 'Does it Matter' that the
Church of England – through the General Synod – has
come to a particular decision, and 'Does it matter' what
action I take as a result of this decision. I've tried to deal
with the first question already – I've tried to indicate
why for some of us it does seem to matter very much
that the Church of England has acted as it has. Now I
would like to address the second question – does it matter
what action I take in response to that decision. Bearing
in mind, I should add, that the decision to ordain women
to the priesthood is for myself and for many others not
the sole or even central cause of our concern. That
decision was in a sense symbolic, it symbolised a whole
drift in the 'official' thinking of the Anglican Church,
a drift towards theological liberalism, towards a whole
'loosening up' of doctrinal and moral standards. A

drift which has followed the casting-off from the safe anchorage of revealed Christianity as it has been traditionally accepted. The decision to ordain women was symbolic, and also it seemed to many of us to be not only a symbol but also both the last straw so far as we were concerned, and the beginning of a new phase in Anglican thinking, with such matters as Lay presidency at the Eucharist just around the corner. But did it matter whether or not we opted out at this point? And more particularly, did whatever action we might or might not take matter to God? After all, he has the whole universe to take care of, and responsibility for countless millions of souls. He works, as the hundred and eighty gallons of wine at Cana reminded us, on a vast scale – and necessarily so.

So do the details of a person's religious life, of their individual religious belief and practice, matter to God? It is an important question, because if the answer is negative, then life becomes somewhat simpler for us all, and certainly no croquet lawns and panelled drawing rooms need ever be abandoned in the cause of conscience! Well for a start there is certainly no difficulty in believing that God cares about us as individuals, notwithstanding his cosmic responsibilities. As we have thought already, it is quite evident that God has created us as individuals and not on any kind of conveyor belt, and this perception is reinforced by Jesus' parables of the lost sheep and the lost coin – the individual sheep and the individual coin which have been found missing being sought for with diligence. And then those two seminal parables of the Good Samaritan and the Prodigal Son, they too speak of how the welfare of the individual matters to God. So what becomes of us, in this life and for eternity, does matter, and so too do the actions we perform and the attitudes we adopt. The parable of the Good Samaritan was given in order that we might learn how we must act towards one another – 'Go and do likewise', and at least one of the purposes of the parable of the Prodigal Son was to teach us how we must be ready to forgive one another. God cares that we love our neighbour as he cares about our personal welfare – this is perfectly clear. But do the doctrinal beliefs we hold matter?

Many would say not. Jesus, they would argue, accepted the Samaritan as he did the Jew. Jesus, they would remind us, taught that at the final judgement we will be deemed worthy or unworthy of heaven according to whether or not we loved our brothers and sisters by feeding them when they were hungry, clothing them when they were naked, visiting them when they were in prison, and welcoming them when they were strangers. There is no suggestion in the important parable of the Sheep and the Goats that judgement will be based upon right belief, and even St Paul, not especially favoured by those of a theologically liberal persuasion, would seem to be reinforcing this when in his celebrated hymn in praise of love, he declares that without love we are worth nothing, even though we may 'know every hidden truth'. So does it matter whether one is a Catholic or a Protestant? Is it, for that matter, significant whether one is a Christian or a Muslim? There are always those ready to tell us that religions are 'all the same', and who are ready to put in a good word for God by saying that he doesn't mind what we are. 'Bloom where you have been planted', an old lady used to say to me, 'don't even consider changing your religious affiliation. Do your best where you are; that's all that matters, that's all that God is asking of you. If God wanted you to be a Roman Catholic you'd have been born one'.

So is God interested, do the details of our religious life matter? The huge quantity of wine at Cana certainly speaks of the largeness of God's working, the vastness of his concerns, and the immensity of that love which we are to accept and radiate. But, as we have seen, this is matched by Our Lord's intimate understanding and care for the individual. A depth of care and concern which must surely involve an interest in what is believed, and in the details of how the spiritual life (which is primarily about the keeping of the first and great commandment that we should love God with all our heart and soul and mind) is lived. Christ is the Word, the one who is made flesh so that he might reveal God; reveal the Truth, show us the Way, and all this so that we might have Life. The Christ of Cana who knew and understood how the bride and bridegroom felt, knows and is concerned with every part of our thinking and feeling. And further, we believe that in his infinite love and wisdom he has a particular plan for each one of us. Our task as disciples is to be sensitive in discerning that plan and that purpose, so that we may act in accordance with it. I find myself believing firmly that God is interested in our religious belief and practice. And more than this, that we will only find that inner peace which comes from living in accordance with his purpose for us if we follow precisely where we perceive him to be leading us. So I don't feel that in leaving the Church of England in order to become a Catholic I am doing something which doesn't matter, and which is of no interest to God. Rather I believe that I am being obedient to that plan and purpose which, in his love, he has for me.

8. *Fill the Jars with Water*

WE do not know what the servants thought when Jesus made this request. Did they think it odd? – surely they must have done: what was the point? Did they consider it merely a waste of time? Did they grumble about those trips to and fro to the well in the heat of the day, raising such a large quantity of water? And did they maybe think that perhaps they'd misheard or misunderstood what the man had said: he couldn't really have said that, could he? Perhaps they'd got it wrong; surely he hadn't asked them to do such a mad thing as this?

So why, I wonder, did they actually do what Jesus asked them, filling the great stone jars with water? Was it simply because they were servants, used to doing what they were told and used sometimes to doing things which didn't seem to have much point? Or was it perhaps because Mary had prepared them for doing something strange when she had said to them a moment ago 'do whatever he tells you'? Or was it because when Jesus gave the order, he spoke with such a note of authority that it would have been nigh impossible to have done anything other than what he said? Later on in his ministry the crowds would comment on, and applaud, the air of authority with which he spoke, and the disciples would marvel that even the wind and the waves obeyed him. Or on a more mundane level, were the servants maybe prepared to do anything and try anything in this crisis situation of the wine having run out in the middle of the celebrations?

Probably it was a mixture of these things which persuaded the servants to do as Jesus requested, and thereby to make what Newman called a 'venture of faith': to act, even though they couldn't possibly see the outcome or even the point of what they were doing. To take a chance, to step out into the dark, with no certainty that what was proposed would achieve anything. And in taking this action, just possibly to be wondering all the time whether they had simply misunderstood what Jesus had said: to be wondering whether they were wasting their time and energy after all.

The whole Christian life of course is just such a venture of faith, a stepping out into the dark with no ultimate assurance that what we are doing in being disciples of Jesus makes sense. Indeed we can't even know for certain that there is a God; if we could, there would be no agnostics or atheists. In the act of believing, and in accepting the consequences of our belief for what we do and say and think, we are making a venture of faith. We are taking a chance and indeed taking a risk. However the risk that we take is not uncalculated, and neither is our belief unreasonable, even though reason alone cannot verify religious belief. We have, we would rightly say, good grounds for accepting the truths of the Christian Faith; those teachings are not irrational, indeed they provide a reasonable interpretation of existence, and they are backed by a very great deal of religious experience. There certainly is risk, the taking of a chance, but this is what faith is about: about trusting, after having weighed things up and having made a decision. This is true faith, reasonable faith, as contrasted with 'blind' faith, where there is no weighing up of things, but just an unreasoned and maybe unreasonable commitment. By faith, we trust God rather as we might trust a friend, having first observed and experienced that friend, and having come to feel that there are satisfactory grounds for our trust. But then our whole life is based upon calculated risks and reasonable suppositions; it's not just in the sphere of religion that we operate in this way.

Just as the whole life of a Christian is a venture of faith, so too there are an infinite number of lesser ventures within the whole. A multitude of occasions when our faith leads us to 'take a chance' as God the Holy Spirit challenges us to take courses of action which are unexpected and even alarming, and whose outcome is uncertain. It may be simply to speak to someone or make a visit. It maybe to use our resources in some unforeseen way. Or it maybe to allow our life to take a new direction. In these situations where we find ourselves challenged to make ventures of faith, we have to rather 'feel our way', or more properly allow ourselves to be led by the Holy Spirit. But often we quail when these demands are made, and wonder as perhaps the servants at Cana wondered, whether we have maybe misheard. Or further, in our case, whether perhaps there is a God at all, or whether we are completely mad. All this belongs to the dangerous, risky, living which the Christian is called to embrace. It belongs in fact to being a servant of God, and as such it is to be accepted with a light heart. 'Fill the jars with water': don't ask why, just do what the Master says!

* * *

It is now more than eighteen months since I began think-ing about leaving the Church of England to become a Roman Catholic, eight months since I made a decision, a fortnight since I left my parish, and hopefully I will be received as a Catholic in six days time. But I still feel a certain amount of surprise at the course my life is taking, and this mingled with a degree of apprehension. I am pretty sure, almost certain, that this is what God has told me to do, but it still seems rather odd and strange. After all, I've been an Anglican since my birth nearly half a century ago, and for half that time I've been minis-tering as a priest. I've borne, I suppose, a certain amount of responsibility in the Anglican Church: the care of souls was entrusted to me by the bishop when I was inducted as parish priest of Walsingham, and twelve years later as parish priest at Wymondham; again I was a member of the General Synod and of the Diocesan Synod and of various diocesan committees. Now I'm to leave all this behind and begin my church-life afresh. Can this really be what God is asking me to do? Have I maybe misheard him? Did I first of all fail to hear what he was saying through the vote taken by the General Synod, and have I now compounded the error by imagining that he has told me to take this particular (and maybe peculiar) course of action? Have I got it all wrong, have I – to be rather melodramatic – pressed the self-destruct button in my life which is now, during the course of the next few years, going to disintegrate?

Taking a grip on myself and looking at the position coolly, I'm not surprised that doubts such as these rise to the surface every so often. For that is how it is when we are led by the Holy Spirit to make ventures of faith; doubts, uncertainties, hesitations, of course these will rise to the surface, and it would be strange – and maybe not a venture of faith at all – if they didn't. But I know that I'm not acting with 'blind' faith in taking this step; what I am doing is not irrational, having no foundation in thought and in experience. Being responsive to God's strange request has most certainly involved my mind, and rightly so because that is part of the equipment which God has given me to enable me to discover his truth and his will. In intellectual terms I can say why I am making this move, indeed I've tried to do this in summary form in preceding chapters. I'm doing more than following a hunch, and still less, I hope, am I following a whim. Perhaps immediately after the Synod vote there was an element of 'All right, let them keep their flaming Church of England, I'm getting out', but this purely emotional reaction was quickly over, and is certainly no part of my thinking now.

But whilst I have tried to use my head in responding to God's request, there have certainly been what might be labelled non-rational factors at work, just as there must have been in the servants' decision to do as Jesus said and fill the six stone jars with water. Becoming a Catholic has somehow 'felt' right, and I was again very strongly aware of this when I attended Mass this morning: I felt very much 'at home', that I was 'where I belonged', that I was becoming planted in soil that was native, and in which I could flourish. Again – and I don't think this is an irrelevant factor, just as it has not been an overriding factor – I have found this proposed course of action attractive in various ways. Attractive rather than repellant – I have felt no antipathy towards the

path I was being asked to take. I have long believed that
one of the tests of a vocation is whether the particular
vocation appeals in some way or another to the person
involved. For whilst God often asks us to do things which
are difficult, he rarely asks us to do things which are
completely and totally alien to the kind of person which
he has made us by creation and by the path along which
he has led us in the past. Further, I have been encouraged
by the fact that a considerable number of friends whose
judgement I trust have said that they think I am doing
the right thing, and even more so by the fact that some
of those friends have taken or are taking just the same
course themselves.

All in all, this odd request that I should become a
Catholic seems to me to come from God, and to demand
that I should boldly and confidently make a venture of
faith. I don't think I've misheard; rather I think that
I've heard perfectly well. So bring out the water jars!
I'm ready to fill them and see what God will do!

9. *The Water now Turned into Wine*

AT CANA, as on the hillside on a later occasion, Jesus took what was available. On the hillside, it was the meagre offering of five loaves and two fishes, which he would use to feed a crowd of five thousand people. At Cana it was water. By taking the loaves and the fish and by taking the water, Jesus acknowledged that they were good. It is true that as part of the creation brought into being by a wise and loving God they could not be otherwise. But Jesus who is that God, the divine Word 'through whom all things came to be' by taking and using these simple things, water, bread, fish, affirmed their goodness; he was not despising them, but rather using them as the physical foundation of his miraculous action.

Then taking at Cana what is good, and what is indeed life-giving – water is especially vital and precious in a hot country – he turns it into what is even better. The water becomes wine, it is enriched. Here at the beginning of his Gospel St John wishes to present Jesus to us as the One who Transforms, and who in the work of transformation, enriches. The Christ who comes not just so that we may have life, but have it more abundantly, and who is powerful to bring about this enrichment. We sing in an ancient office hymn for the season of Epiphany that Jesus 'Gives at Cana this for sign, the water reddens into wine': the miracle at Cana is a sign that the Christ who transforms, and who in transforming enriches, is present in the midst of his people.

This first of the Signs in the Fourth Gospel also points forward, as we have seen, to the last and greatest of the Signs, the Resurrection of Our Lord, and in addition to pointing towards it, also prepares us to understand it. In resurrection the human body, wonderful (but limited) as it is, is transformed and enriched just as the water at Cana was. The flesh which Jesus had taken of Mary at the Incarnation was good, the sinless flesh taken of a sinless mother, and by the time that this flesh was laid in the tomb it had been used for the very highest purposes, used as an instrument in the revelation of God to his people and in that self-offering whereby Our Lord made atonement for us. Good, holy, infinitely precious: and yet by resurrection that flesh was made yet more glorious. By that transformation which we call resurrection the body of Jesus was invested with endless life and prepared for being taken up to the throne of heaven. Resurrection is the promise which is made to us as disciples of the risen Christ. For Mary this promise has already been fulfilled, at the glorious assumption which followed her death; for us, it will be fulfilled on the Last Day, when God by his divine power will take the dust and ashes to which our bodies have been reduced and from them will make us the spiritual body of the resurrection. The enrichment of water into wine at Cana not only points forward to the transformation of Our Lord's body at the first Easter, but also to our own resurrection at the Last Day.

This present body of ours, this mortal body, is wonderful. Its physical and mental capabilities are amazing. To be able to walk, to see, to hear, to think, to understand – these are great things, and to the ear of faith they proclaim our divine authorship, the fact that we are made by a wise and loving God. But the resurrection body with which we will be clothed on the Last Day, when the saving work of Jesus comes to completion, and our body no less than our soul knows the fullness of redemption, this resurrection body will be infinitely more precious than our present body. Wine likewise is superior to water; water is good, one of the best gifts of God. But wine is even better. Water sustains, but wine is the bringer of joy – hence the crisis at the marriage celebration at Cana. No one would have died of thirst at Cana whilst there was water to drink. But there would not have been a party. And so therefore Our Lord's work of transformation and enrichment at Cana. He wants us here and now to begin to experience the joy of his kingdom in heaven. And so at Cana he enriched water into wine, and now at the altar he enriches bread and wine into his Body and Blood. Just as one day he will enrich us to be citizens of the new Jerusalem.

* * *

When, by being received next Saturday, I become a full member of the Catholic Church, I will have to start being very careful concerning what I say about other denominations. Because in these ecumenical days we must not be found criticising one another. So maybe only now, in these twenty days in between my leaving Wymondham on July 31st and my being received on August 20th – these strange days when I'm not certain whether I'm technically an Anglican or a Roman Catholic-in-waiting – perhaps only now dare I liken the Church of England to water and the Roman Catholic Church to wine!

But bearing in mind what has been said above, I'm clearly not denigrating the Church of England when I liken it to water. Water is good, precious, life-giving, and I'm deeply aware that during my near half-century as an Anglican I have received abundant grace, both sacramental and non-sacramental. I came to life as a Christian within the Church of England, and there is so much in the past for which I am grateful. When my resignation from Wymondham was announced it was reported, not surprisingly, in the local regional paper. I hadn't spoken to any reporter, but the opening lines of the piece referred to me as 'Disillusioned Priest'. I resented that, as I don't think of myself in those terms. In so far as I had disagreed with the path being taken by the Church of England, 'Disagreeable Priest' would have been more acceptable! I don't feel disillusioned with the Anglican Church any more than I feel dismissive of it, or have any wish or intention of disparaging it. Obviously I have become increasingly aware of its limitations. It is not the whole Church, nor, I would now say, has it the mark of wholeness. But like water, it is still good.

What then are the qualities which this water has and so what am I particularly sad to leave? First perhaps, its history, a history which I've had opportunities to study at various times and which I've found both fascinating and edifying. Then within this history, and an essential part of it, are the numerous people who have inspired me and who indeed have been my heroes: people such as Thomas Ken and John Keble, known for their holiness; people like Lancelot Andrewes and Edward Pusey, renowned for their scholarship; people like Henry Scott Holland and Alfred Hope Patten, who were considerable personalities; distinguished Anglicans I've known personally, such as G. W. O. Addleshaw and E. L. Mascall. The names flood into my mind, and I feel sad and more than sad to be moving in a sense out of communion with the people who have played such an important part in my religious development. In one way, history belongs to all of us, and yet there is a sense in which it belongs more especially to the particular denomination whose own history it is. Then second, I admire and see as part of the characteristic goodness of the Church of England its choral and liturgical tradition, and linked with this the architectural setting of its worship. I suppose in part I'm talking now about the aesthetic heritage of the Anglican Church, but not just that. Not, of course, that every Anglican place of worship has dignified ceremonial and fine music being offered to God in beautiful surroundings! Far from it, and it is possible to cap every horror story about Roman Catholic worship with at least one from the Church of England. But I think it is possible that the Church of England has more centres of excellence as regards liturgical presentation than the Catholic Church has, and possibly it is more successful – at least here and there – at maintaining that important element of awe and reverence in its worship. I believe that the Church of England at its best – and for me that usually means the Anglo-Catholic wing of it – is very good indeed. I sometimes used to be asked what 'High Church' meant, and I would reply that being High Church means having a high view of the Spiritual Life, of the Sacraments and of Prayer, public and private, and that in a High Church parish one would find that the clergy tried to maintain a High standard of teaching, of worship, and of pastoral care. I think that in the history of the Church, Anglicanism at its best with its scholarship and its holiness – and more particularly Anglicanism as it was before its recent reorientation in a liberal direction – will always command respect. Traditional Anglicanism certainly continues to command my respect, and, as I've said, I am far from belittling it when I compare it to good, fresh, wholesome water.

Jesus took water at Cana, and I believe that he is taking me, and that he will likewise change and enrich me through my life as a Catholic. For I believe that if the Church of England can be compared to water – good, but with certain limitations – so the Catholic Church can be compared with wine. I would like to say more about this in the following chapter. But one matter which I would like to comment on here is the fact that the 'me' who Christ is taking is a priest, and being a priest has been central to my life. It can't be other than that to someone who believes that he has this special vocation from God, and that Holy Orders have been entrusted to him. It is a well-known fact of course that the Roman Catholic Church does not acknowledge Anglican Orders: indeed the Bull issued by Pope Leo XIII in 1896, *Apostolicae Curae*, declared Anglican Orders to be 'null and void'. Friends not unreasonably ask me how I feel about this aspect of becoming a Catholic – the fact that my Anglican orders will not be recognised. How does one deal with this? I think maybe the first thing to say is that the question of Orders cannot be a deciding factor as regards whether or not an Anglican priest becomes a Catholic: the deciding factor of course is the awareness that Our Lord through his Holy Spirit is leading one in a particular direction. There is a sense too in which it is right to leave the whole matter in the hands of God and his Church, and I don't think that this is irresponsible. Rather it is a recognition that Holy Orders are bestowed by God through his Church, and are never any kind of personal possession, 'belonging' to the individual priest. But having said that, those of us Anglican priests who are becoming Catholics at the present time are greatly helped by the fact that far from being asked to deny our past ministry as Anglican priests, we are rather being encouraged to celebrate and give thanks for that ministry. And as regards the re-ordination which some of us hope to undergo in the future, well, at least one Roman Catholic bishop has told people in our position to think of this as being primarily a 'topping up', a 'supplying of whatever might be lacking'. I for one am very happy to see any eventual re-ordination in this way, and also I would see an important element in such a re-ordination as a coming into communion with universal priesthood of the Church – a communion which at present I manifestly do not enjoy. I cannot deny my Anglican Orders; I would find it difficult to say that I am not already a priest. But I'm not asked to do that; only to recognise, as I certainly do, that my Orders cannot be considered regular insofar as they were bestowed by a bishop who was not in communion with the See of Peter. I ask only that Christ will take me, as he did the water at Cana, and make of me what he will.

Water sustains, and I have been spiritually sustained by the Church of England during what must be the major part of my earthly pilgrimage. But wine does more than sustain, it brings joy. Others have told me of the happiness which they have discovered as members of the Catholic Church, and I feel certain that I too will come to experience a new outpouring of the gifts of the Holy Spirit, and not least amongst them the gift of holy joy.

10. *You have Left the Good Wine until Now*

I SUSPECT that when we read St John's account of the marriage at Cana we don't give too much thought to the fact that the second lot of wine, the water which Jesus had transformed into wine, was judged better than the wine which had been drunk before. 'Well it would be, wouldn't it?' is our natural reaction; 'Jesus made it, it was his working, so of course it would be better.' We simply accept the fact that the best wine was the wine which resulted from the miracle: that is just how we would suppose it to be. But isn't this to forget that Jesus is the Word 'through whom all things came to be'? And as the creative Word of God, the one who is the cause of all that is and whose work of creation is never ending, isn't Jesus just as much the maker of the first wine, brought into being by natural means, as he is the second, brought into being miraculously? Isn't it fundamentally wrong for us to equate God's 'normal' working, his work-ing in accordance with those laws of nature which he has laid down, with *vin ordinaire*, whilst equating the occasions when he chooses to suspend those laws with chateau bottled? Are not both modes of the divine working equally wonderful?

Therefore I don't think that we can just dismiss the fact that the 'miraculous' wine was the best as being inevitable; there must be more to it than that. Perhaps in drawing attention to the fact that the second wine was the best St John is reminding us of the generosity of the Christ, who adds grace to grace – 'to those who have shall yet more be given' – in that he not only resolves the crisis which arose at the marriage feast by providing additional wine, but in addition, this new wine was the very best. But maybe a more important significance which St John wants us to grasp is that for the Christian, who is in the process of being redeemed and sanctified and whose redemption will come to perfection in heaven, the best must always lie ahead. In physical and perhaps in mental terms, our life may be seen as a steady and rather depressing deterioration after a certain point, as our limbs and senses and maybe our brain gradually become impaired. But for the believer this is not the whole or the essential story. Hopefully our salvation is being worked out, and by the constant bestowal of grace we are deepening that union with God which will come to fruition in the future, reaching its culmination in our resurrection on the Last Day. So that as seen by the eyes of faith, the best wine is that which will follow, and it will come to us through the working of Christ our Saviour, who made wonderfully good wine at Cana after the first, inferior wine, had all been drunk.

There are a couple of things about the steward which seem noteworthy. One is that he only recognised the excellence and indeed the superiority of the second lot of wine because he had already tasted the first. He may at the outset have thought that the first wine was quite good, and certainly adequate for the occasion. There is no reason to suppose that whilst the first, natural, wine was circulating the steward was critical of it and thinking all the time how dreadful it was. It was only when he tasted the new, supernatural, wine that he came to see the inadequacy of the first; it was by contrasting the two that he came to see their relative merits, and to see quite clearly that the second wine was the best. We find in the spiritual life that discernment comes with experience, and often by the means of contrast. It begins perhaps by our realisation that the explanation which Christian teaching gives for why the earth exists and for why we human beings exist, is more adequate than any other that we may have considered. It continues, maybe, with our perception that the Christian way of living is superior to any alternative kind of living, based either on other principles or on none. And hopefully we also discover, by means of contrast, that life lived in union with God has a richness as well as a meaning, that is superior to anything else. It is by contrast that we discover what is best, just as the steward at the marriage did by contrasting the two wines.

The other thing which we might notice about the steward, and which carries on from the first, is that he was discerning: he discerned the contrast between the first wine and the second. He might not have bothered tasting either of the wines, he might simply have concerned himself with the arrangements for serving them, and not stopped to see what they were like, and to consider their relative merits. Or, having drunk them both he might have tossed them down without bothering to stop and think how they tasted in comparison with each other. He might have been totally undiscerning. But no, here was a man who had discernment, and who used his senses and his mind to arrive at a judgement. He was alert to discover truth. In just the same way the Christian must be discerning, ready to see and recognise God's working and God's truth, and to work out its implications for the individual. It is as easy in the realm of spiritual things as in any other to be blind or at least unperceptive, but the disciple, Jesus taught, must be alert. Ready to read and understand the signs of the times, ready above all else to recognise and respond to God's will. It is important that we use the means of discernment which God has given us, so that we too may recognise and enjoy the best wine.

*   *   *

As I prepare for life as a member of the Catholic Church – and my reception is now only four days away – I certainly feel that in my life of faith the best wine has been kept until now. Earlier I compared the Church of England to water, the good water which Jesus took and miraculously transformed into good wine; maybe a better comparison would have been the ordinary wine which the guests drank earlier, the wine which was adequate at the time and which served its purpose, but which finally ran out, and was found in retrospect to have been lacking in excellence. Well maybe this seems hard and unkind, but I have set myself to be completely honest. I set down what is no more than my own opinion, and I certainly wish only to speak the truth in love.

Pursuing this new analogy between the original wine at the wedding and the Church of England, I suppose I can now say that like the steward at Cana I have tasted both wines. For having lived all my life hitherto as an Anglican, I have now in the past few months had the opportunity to study the teaching and practice of the Catholic Church, and then more recently there has been the opportunity to join in its worship and fellowship. Again like the steward, I have observed a contrast, and further I have come to the opinion, as he did, that the one is to be preferred to the other. For me, as for the steward, the best wine seems to have been kept until now. But as I contrast the two churches, what are the merits which seem to make the one superior to the other? Why do I feel that this second wine is better, and what features of it do I expect to enjoy especially? I think I would want to concentrate on four things. Most if not all of the four things have already been mentioned singly, but it might be useful to place them here together, as complementary characteristics of the new wine, since together they have led me to think the new wine is more excellent than the old.

A first characteristic which attracts me is the fact that the Catholic Church has a strong teaching authority; it both knows and says what it believes, and there seems to be a refreshing lack of wooliness in what it says about matters of doctrine and morality. It doesn't blunt what it says by a thousand qualifications and 'but thens' or 'maybes'. Nor is it afraid to say what 'the world' finds unpalatable and uncomfortable. Christ through the Holy Spirit is the one who comforts his people, but also he is the one who challenges and disturbs, the one whom some went away from because they didn't like his teaching and couldn't accept it. The Catholic Church doesn't seem concerned first and foremost to please, and to say only what is acceptable. Rather it proclaims the truth as it has received it and understood it, irrespective of whether offence will be given. It seeks only, to my mind, to be faithful to the Gospel of the risen Christ, and to fearlessly communicate his teaching. I know that to some this clear strong teaching seems narrow, too 'black or white', and not to take sufficient account of the complexity both of human beings and their relationships, and indeed of the essential mystery which surrounds being and truth. Yet the mighty and mysterious Word was made flesh – God communicated with his people in a clear and concrete way. The Truth was made apparent, and if we are to begin to know God and know how he wants us to live and act, then it needs to be. The Catholic Church speaks clearly, and its teaching authority has, necessarily, a shape and a centre. The fact that it is centred upon the papacy gives it coherence, and accords with Our Lord's charge to Peter to 'feed his sheep'.

Then a second good characteristic is the fact that the whole life of the Catholic Church is centred upon the Mass. In view of the fact that worship is the primary function of the Church, and the Mass is the chief act of Christian worship – the one act of worship commanded by Our Lord himself – this seems to be wholly right and good. And so at the heart of the life of the Catholic Church is that loving of God which finds its most natural expression in worship, together with the offering of Our Lord's saving work, and the very fountain of grace which is the life of the risen and ascended Christ made present to us in the Sacrament of Holy Communion. Day by day the Mass is celebrated, and not in the odd Catholic Church here and there where the priest happens to think it matters, but in churches everywhere. And Sunday by Sunday Catholics gather together not just perhaps to take part in the offering of the Mass, or maybe alternatively in the choral rendering of an office or maybe in some form of spiritual light entertainment, but always, Sunday by Sunday, to take part in the one service that Jesus asked us to celebrate, and to receive that sacramental grace which we need if we are to go out into the world to live out his Gospel. It makes sense, and it seems to be so obviously in accordance with Our Lord's will, that the Mass should be at the centre of the Church's life, just as it has been from the beginning. It also seems deeply and profoundly right that in the Catholic Church the Sacraments are given their proper place. Their part in God's plan for our salvation is crucial, they are necessary elements in the way in which he has chosen to bring about our redemption and sanctification. It can never be right for them to be neglected and considered to be of merely secondary importance.

For me a third characteristic of the good wine which is the Catholic Church would be the universality, the catholicity, of that Church. The simple but so significant fact that you can go anywhere in the world and find fellow Christians with whom you share a similar allegiance and a common liturgy, and with whom you are in full communion; fellow Christians with whom you join as members of the one body in receiving and proclaiming the one Christ. Our Lord prayed earnestly for the oneness of his Church, and there seems to be a particular authenticity about the Christian body which so obviously has the best claim to be the heart and centre of Christendom.

Finally, a further characteristic of the Catholic Church which makes it seem to me to be the best wine is the fact that there is a marked degree of unanimity within it. I am well aware that there are many areas in which Roman Catholics hold differing and indeed conflicting views – not least in the matter of the ordination of women to the priesthood. The Catholic Church of today is certainly not the monolithic structure which it was formerly perceived to be, with no one stepping out of a very strict line as regards worship and doctrine. It is said that in the past some people converted to Catholicism because the old very solid uniformity appealed to them; certainly an informed convert of today knows that he or she will not be required or allowed to switch-off mentally, and surrender entirely to a narrowly defined set of propositions. And yet for all this, to the Anglican the Catholic Church does seem to have a level of unanimity which is markedly different to what the convert has experienced hitherto. Despite whatever differences of opinion there may be in a group of Catholics, one is still aware of a common sense of purpose and identity; of a shared faith and of belonging to the same body, with a common loyalty based upon an essentially common mind. Sometimes the comprehensiveness of the Church of England is not only commended but is even called its 'glory'; to others of us it seems a debilitating weakness, and to effectively prevent that feeling of being part of one people, one family, which is so basic and indeed precious a part of living as a member of the people of God. The psalmist declared it to be a good and joyful thing for brethren to dwell together in unity; I feel that he too would find the essential unanimity within the Catholic Church a characteristic which marks it out as the best wine.

I hope that like the steward at Cana I have been alert to the situation in which I have found myself; that I have marked the contrast between the two churches correctly, and that I have discerned rightly which of the two seems to be most in accordance with how God wants his Church to be. Perhaps those who disagree with me will repeat proverbs about the far off hills being green, and the grass being greener on the other side of the fence. Well green is certainly the colour of life and of growth, and whether I and others grow and flourish spiritually in the Catholic Church will remain to be seen. I can only say that at present I feel very certain which of the wines I want to be served!

11. *The First of the Signs by which Jesus Revealed his Glory*

'THE WORD became flesh; he came to dwell amongst us, and we saw his glory, such glory as befits the Father's only Son, full of grace and truth.' So writes St John in the Prologue to his Gospel, and his belief that the divine glory has been shown forth in Jesus is one of the central convictions underlying his Gospel. Glory, St John says, is revealed in the Incarnation itself, in the divine Word taking flesh of a human mother and thereby joining our common humanity to his divinity. It is seen too in the death of Jesus upon the Cross, and it is also seen in the Signs, or miracles, which Jesus performed: in particular St John speaks of the changing of water into wine and the raising of the dead Lazarus as being occasions when glory was made manifest.

But what does St John mean by glory? Clearly not the kind of conventional splendour which we most readily associate with the word, no armies, gold, or trumpets, still less squadrons of angels and flashings of lightning. It is no earthly or even celestial glory which St John refers to when he speaks of glory being revealed: it is nothing less than the very nature of God himself which is shown forth – the glory of the divine being. And what is the essential characteristic of that being? St John makes it clear in his first Letter: 'God is love; and his love was disclosed to us in this, that he sent his only Son into the world to bring us life'.

Love is essential to the nature of God, and so if the glory which is revealed in Christ is a showing of the divine nature, then that glory which is made manifest is nothing other than the love of God. If then glory is to be understood in terms of divine love, we see very clearly how the Incarnation itself, the death on the Cross, and the miracles are revelatory of love. We remember that it was solely out of love for fallen man that God the Son took our common humanity; he became man, he was made incarnate, in order that he might redeem the humanity which he had taken and restore to us the inheritance of eternal life which had been forfeited by the disobedience of mankind. Here in the Incarnation was the burning unselfish love of God, and this was further disclosed by Our Lord's death on the Cross. 'Greater love has no man than this, that a man should lay down his life for his friends' . . . in the preparedness of Jesus to suffer and to die for us we see very clearly the depths of the divine love, which makes the crucifixion a particular showing of that glory which is the love of God. And then in the miracles too we see the divine love, and most obviously in the motivation of them. St John almost seems to suggest that these were set pieces, staged for the purpose of evoking belief in the onlookers. But this cannot be the whole story. Surely there is also an element of spontaneous reaction to a situation in which help was needed, a reaction which is brought about through Jesus' love for those who stood in need of his powerful intervention (and this, I suppose, being a kind of microcosm of his loving intervention to redeem lost and fallen humanity). So that at Bethany, it was love for the sorrowing sisters which led Jesus to restore their brother to them, and at Cana, love for the disconsolate bride and bridegroom which led him to save their marriage feast from disaster by providing extra wine. In these miracles we see manifestations of the divine love operative in ordinary human situations, just as in a wider field we see it revealed in the Incarnation and the death on the Cross. In these showings of the divine love, the glory, the very nature of God, is made known to us.

Whenever we encounter Jesus, whenever he comes to us in the life of prayer which we are called to lead, or in the Word and Sacraments which he has given to his Church, or in the lives and faces of those people who are living close to him, then it is the love of God which is made manifest to us. For every coming of Our Lord is a coming in love, just as it is also a coming in judgement

and in mercy. He is to us in our own situation just what
he was to the bride and bridegroom at Cana – the one
who understands our needs and who is never indifferent
to them. The one who is powerful to come to our assist-
ance, and this very often in wholly unexpected ways. The
Christ who reveals himself to us is the one who shows
us the love of God, and who in doing so discloses to us
the very nature, the glory, of God. He discloses himself
to us so that we by redemption and sanctification may
come to share in that glory – so that we, when we come
to perfection, may love as he loves us, sharing thereby
in the very being of God.

*   *   *

In the past few weeks a number of kind friends have
written to me, and most of them have combined good
wishes and the assurance of prayers with expressions of
sympathy. They say how they've felt for me; that they're
sure I must have gone through agonies in making my
decision to leave the Church of England, that the process
of leaving my parish must have been painful, and that my
last Sunday at Wymondham must have been distressing.
Anguish is a word that some have used. I've found these
expressions which people have written, I know, out of
the kindness of their hearts, embarrassing. And this
because they make me feel a complete and utter fraud.
The fact is that I have not felt any agony, pain, distress,
or anguish at all. There have, naturally, been odd
moments when I have asked myself whether I am doing
the right thing; whether I have acted correctly, or
whether I have misheard God and made a ghastly mistake. But only moments. Most of the time I have experienced only what I am experiencing now, namely a feeling
of complete assurance and peace. Actually this surprises
me as much as it surprises my friends. Like them, I
would have expected the process of leaving the Anglican
Church and joining the Catholic Church to be traumatic,
but the fact is that it hasn't been. At least not yet!

The ease with which I seem to be making the transition, with an almost total freedom from anxiety and
distress, seems to stem largely from the fact that what I

ought to do has become perfectly clear to me over the last eighteen months or so. Again friends assume that I've spent many hours in thought and prayer as I've sought to discover the way forward. But again I have to admit that this has not really been the case. I have just seemed to know with more or less complete certainty what I must do; I feel that God has made his will very plain. And then having been shown what to do, I've been given the further grace of the will to do it, and the ability to do it cheerfully and without pain and regrets. I have the strongest feeling that I've been led, led almost as a child is led. And this feeling has been heightened by the fact that all kinds of practical difficulties, mostly to do with leaving a large house and dealing with its contents, have, without exception, resolved themselves in a wholly satisfactory way and without undue worry.

Now all of this – being shown God's will, being given grace to comply with it, and having had the way of complying with it made so clear, both emotionally and practically – all of this has been for me a wonderful revelation of the love of God. A showing of his love for me, and hence a manifestation in my life of his very nature, of his glory. I have experienced this love in the guidance and care which I believe God has given me directly, and also I have experienced that same divine love as it has been mediated through the various people who have shown care and concern for me in this time of transition. I've mentioned the understanding and support which I received from my parishioners at Wymondham, people who could so easily have shown resentment and disappointment; I've mentioned too the kindness and concern of my friends, who have offered various kinds of practical help; and now as I prepare for my reception into the Catholic Church in a couple of days time, I'm amazed and humbled by the good wishes and prayers which I'm receiving from members of the local Catholic community. One of the ways in which God shows us his love is by loving us through the people around us. I have most certainly experienced this, and it has formed an important part of the revelation of divine love which I feel has come to me.

'Jesus revealed his glory and led his disciples to believe in him.' The miracle at Cana, the transformation of water into wine in which Jesus revealed his glory – which is the divine love – was powerful to evoke belief in those who had experienced it. That was its effect; it left them with a deeper acceptance of Jesus as The Christ, the one who is both sent from God and who is God, the divine Word. It enabled them to commit themselves more deeply to him, and to trust him more completely. Like those first disciples, I too feel that I have experienced in a small way the glory, the love, of God, and I too feel that this has led me to a deeper faith. I believe that I am now a somewhat less proud, self-assertive, and materialistic person than I was, and that in the future I will be able to live my life in a greater spirit of trust and commitment. I think and I hope that the particular revelation of glory which God has granted me will enable me to respond with a greater love to the love which he has shown for me.

12. *After this He went Down to Capernaum*

AND so the time came when it was all over. The wine had been drunk and the guests had gone home. The first of the Signs had been given, and now the special moment of revelation was passed. The marriage feast had presumably been a huge success – certainly the crisis which threatened to disrupt it had been resolved, and some very fine wine had been served – and as for the disciples of Jesus, their eyes had been opened, and consequently their conviction concerning Jesus had been deepened. Now it was time for things to return to normal for a while, and Jesus together with his mother, his brothers and his disciples went down to Capernaum. There, it seems, nothing much happened, since all that St John can find to say about the time in Capernaum is that they didn't stay there very long.

Perhaps this ending to the story reminds us of the conclusion to the accounts of Our Lord's Transfiguration which we find in the Synoptic Gospels; indeed in some ways the account of the Marriage at Cana, which does not appear in the other Gospels, is almost the equivalent of the Transfiguration, which St John for his part does not record. On the holy mountain, as at Cana, there was a moment of revelation, when the glory of the incarnate Christ was made manifest. And also in both cases the moment of revelation was followed by the inevitable descent back into ordinary life: Jesus and the three disciples 'came down' the holy mountain: after Cana he and his party 'went down to Capernaum'.

This pattern is very familiar, of course, to Christians. All of us who are seeking to lead the spiritual life, and, as disciples of Jesus, to grow in a union with God which will prepare us for the life of heaven – all of us know about the pattern in which times of revelation are succeeded by times of spiritual ordinariness. Sometimes the Cana times, the moments when Jesus reveals his glory to us, seem few and far between. We feel that we would like rather more times of encouragement, in which our faith is supported and deepened. Likewise the Capernaum times sometimes seem to be rather more than just ordinary, they seem positively arid, times of darkness when we are tempted to unbelief and despair. We sometimes cry out with the psalmist 'Has God forgotten to be gracious?' But this seems to be the pattern which God in his wisdom has established for us – times of vision and encouragement followed by times of testing and perseverance, Capernaum following Cana. We obviously need both, else God wouldn't provide both, and certainly we know in our hearts that he is guiding and directing us as is best, shaping us up by spiritual good times and spiritual bad times for life with him in heaven.

Capernaum, where no Sign took place, must have seemed dull after Cana, but ahead of course lay both further Signs, the miraculous healing of limbs, the feeding of crowds, the raising of the dead – more showings of the glory of Christ – and also the events of the Passion and Resurrection. In our own lives there is that pattern we've just considered, with times of revelation alternating with times of spiritual dullness, but also as with Jesus and his disciples there lies ahead for us the particular experiences of pain, death, and resurrection. None of us knows what difficulties and trials we may have to encounter in the future, any more than the disciples knew the difficulties which lay ahead for them as they left Cana, but we are probably right in assuming that our life won't be an endless party. We know too that at some point we are going to be called to follow Our Lord into the experience of death. But with this knowledge goes the assurance that for us as for him death will be followed by resurrection. For that is his promise to us, that at the last the water of our present mortal selves will be transformed and enriched into the new wine of redeemed and recreated humanity, in which we will rejoice for ever in the marriage feast of the Lamb.

*   *   *

I hope to be received into the Roman Catholic Church tomorrow. It will be a new beginning for me, but also it will mark the end of the first and almost certainly the major part of my spiritual pilgrimage. It will also see the ending of a strange interlude in my life, this twenty days since I left my Anglican parish and during which time I've been neither an Anglican nor a Catholic, and have been unable to receive the Sacrament of Holy Communion. But odd though these twenty days have been in some ways, I don't feel that they've been a barren or a wasted time. For one thing I've enjoyed revisiting Cana and contemplating the first of the Signs which Jesus performed. I have learnt about discipleship and faith by listening to and by watching Mary, the servants, the steward, the disciples, and my trust and my sense of wonder have been increased through observing the loving and gracious actions of Our Lord himself. Also the revisiting of Cana has helped me to understand better my own present situation, and to see more clearly what God has been saying to me in recent months, and indeed is saying to me now. I still don't know whether it has been a good idea to set down my personal reflections. They are by the nature of the case somewhat disordered, and lacking in clarity of thought and expression. Some of the opinions which I have stated and judgements which I have made have been arrived at hastily, and may be biased and unfair. On the other hand, there are advantages in immediacy and spontaneity, qualities from which a photograph often benefits. These personal reflections have, I suppose, been a kind of photograph, taken at a particular moment in time. A time of great change in my own life, and this a tiny and insignificant part of a much wider and far-reaching change which is taking place at present in English religion. As I said in the Introduction, the only justification for setting down my thoughts on paper is that they might possibly be of interest or even help to someone else who finds him or herself in a similar situation.

Like the time which the disciples spent at Cana, these last few months have been for me a time of revelation, a time when I have experienced in a new way the glory of God, which is the divine love. I have experienced this in the loving and gentle, but always firm and sure guidance which I have received from him; by the way in which things have not only become so clear but so attainable; and in the kindness and support which I have received from the people around me. But after tomorrow, and once I have become a member of the Catholic Church, I know that I will have to leave Cana and go down into Capernaum, there to commence the ordinary life of a Catholic Christian. I believe that this will be a wholly good experience, something to look forward to eagerly, and I've given my reasons for thinking that this will be the case. I feel certain that I will find in the Catholic Church the love and joy and peace which the Holy Spirit bestows, and that it will be a setting in which I will be able to grow in the love of God and the loving of my brothers and sisters in Christ.

But at the same time I know that I must not see myself as another Alice about to tumble into Wonderland, nor must I suppose that once I am a Catholic it is going to become easy to live the Christian life. I discovered many years ago at my Anglican Confirmation and First Communion that these kind of moments in one's life don't lead to the immediate withdrawal of temptation and doubt, and to the onset of instant peace and holiness! No, I am reasonably free, I hope, from unreal expectations. There will, I hope, be other times in the future when moments of revelation will strengthen and encourage me, just as the witnessing of those subsequent Signs must have strengthened the faith and encouraged the perseverance of the disciples. But I fully realise that most of my life as a Christian disciple will be lived in Capernaum, the place where the living is not so much easy as ordinary, and where the real work of being a disciple of Jesus is carried out. Then also, I expect, there will be times of special difficulty, times when the Cross has to be carried. Maybe certain difficulties – not serious, but real – will come sooner rather than later. Perhaps it will be more difficult than I imagine to adjust to my new life.

Perhaps it will be a kind of bereavement not to have a parish to look after any more – at least for a time – and maybe it will be miserable not to be responsible for the souls of people, young and old, as I have been for the past twenty-four years. Perhaps, again, I will not be re-ordained as a Catholic priest – that is a matter for the Church to decide, and obviously I must abide by its decision – but if this does not happen it would certainly be a sadness, in so far as the priestly ministry is very central to my life. I am sure that for me as for all Christian people there will be difficulties to face, but I know too that for me as for all Christian people the end of the matter will be 'the resurrection of the dead and the life everlasting', and that in company with my brothers and sisters in Christ throughout the world I will be straining forward to those joys which await us.

And so tomorrow with a joyful heart I will be yet another of those people who, in the words of an Oratorian, 'have experienced the movement of grace within their hearts and, laying aside the tradition of their upbringing, have knelt to acknowledge an older and more vital system at the feet of the Vicar of Christ'. I will, I hope, have been true to the leading which God has given me, and I pray that I with all Christian people may always be able to pray with sincerity and obedience 'Thy will be done'.

POSTSCRIPT

I WAS RECEIVED into the Catholic Church yesterday by Bishop Alan Clark, the Bishop of East Anglia, at a Mass held in the chapel adjoining his residence. I particularly appreciated the fact that he was prepared to receive me himself, because I felt that the part which he had played in my perception of God's will had been significant. A week or two after the General Synod vote in November 1992 I had asked to see him, and he had received me with the greatest kindness and sensitivity. He again saw me, at my request, a year later. On neither occasion did he make any attempt to influence my decision, still less to put any kind of pressure on me, whether theological, spiritual, or emotional. I was aware, as were others who sought interviews with him, that he fully understood our situation and our distress, and was genuinely and deeply sympathetic. I remember reading an article somewhere in the press where he was accused of 'collecting' Anglican clergy; it would, I think, be very untrue and unjust to suggest that he had at any stage 'fished' for clergy converts, or even that he particularly encouraged us to change our allegiance. Certainly my own experience was that he simply made himself available, very readily and graciously, to listen and to answer questions, and this in a wholly pastoral and very informal way. Insofar as I and others were influenced by him, it was far more by his attitude towards us which was one of true Christian charity, gentleness, and understanding, than by anything which he specifically said, offered, or suggested. It was the fact that he had been so welcoming in his attitude that had encouraged me to ask if he would be prepared to receive me himself, and I was delighted when he readily agreed to do so.

I felt that the bishop's sensitivity was well reflected by the fact that he had chosen the feast of St Bernard of

Clairvaux for the reception, just as it was in the warm and affectionate welcome which he offered to the dozen or so of my friends who had asked to be present, most of whom were non-Catholics. The very attractive modern chapel was filled with sunlight, and the liturgy was celebrated with simplicity, reverence, and joy. In his homily, the bishop spoke of St Bernard's great love for the Church, and he generously suggested that it was a love for the Church which had prompted me to seek to do God's will by coming into full communion with the universal Church. He spoke too of this feast being a 'feast of love', on which we recall that burning heroic love which St Bernard had for God and for his brothers and sisters in Christ; a love which makes St Bernard so attractive, and a saint with so much to teach Christian people about the Christian way. I will always remember my reception as a moment of deep peace and joy; a moment of grace which will serve, I feel, to sustain me in whatever difficulties may lie ahead.

Then this morning I went to my first Sunday Mass as a Catholic. It didn't seem at all strange or novel to be there, and neither did I feel any particular elation or excitement. I certainly felt very happy and very much at peace, but primarily being there seemed to be entirely natural. I felt I had finally arrived at where I was meant to be, and where I could feel completely at home. When at the beginning of the Mass the priest asked us to be silent for a moment and form our own particular intention, I knew that mine must be one of thanksgiving. Of thanksgiving for all that had happened to me, together with prayer for others, that they too may come to that same feeling of joy and peace in the practice of religion which I was now experiencing.